"It's not uncommon for me to hear friends and members of the church I pastor talk of how 'Christmas snuck up on them.' Paul David Tripp has written a fantastic Advent devotional for individuals or families, and it's the perfect solution for preparing our hearts and homes to celebrate what's really going on underneath the tinsel and the trees."

Matt Chandler, lead teaching pastor, The Village Church; president, Acts29 Church Planting Network

"Paul David Tripp has the rare gift of conveying profound biblical truths in a simple and accessible manner. *Come, Let Us Adore Him* will help you prepare for the arrival of the Christ child on a deep level, no matter where you are currently in life."

William Vanderbloemen, CEO and president, Vanderbloemen Search Group

"Theology serves us best when it is translated into devotion. Paul David Tripp's *Come, Let Us Adore Him* is that rare gem—great theology inspiring great devotion. This book will enrich my family's experience of Christmas this year, and I believe it can enrich your Christmas too."

Ray Ortlund, lead pastor, Immanuel Church, Nashville, Tennessee; council member, The Gospel Coalition; president, Renewal Ministries; author, *Marriage and the Mystery of the Gospel*

"In the chaos, inadequacies, and fears that all too often overshadow the Advent season, it is easy to forget that this day, above all other days, speaks of stillness, welcome, and assurance. It tells us that we have been, and are now, completely loved—no matter if we remember all the presents or if the lights on our tree won't work. This devotional will help us remember the great love with which we have been loved. Read its pages, share it with your family. Enter into that manger scene. And breathe."

Elyse M. Fitzpatrick, author, *Found in Him*

Come, Let Us Adore Him

Other Crossway Books by Paul David Tripp

Awe: Why It Matters for Everything We Think, Say, and Do (2015)

Dangerous Calling: Confronting the Unique Challenges of Pastoral Ministry (2012)

New Morning Mercies: A Daily Gospel Devotional (2014)

Parenting: 14 Gospel Principles That Can Radically Change Your Family (2016)

A Shelter in the Time of Storm: Meditations on God and Trouble (2009)

What Did You Expect? Redeeming the Realities of Marriage (2010)

Whiter Than Snow: Meditations on Sin and Mercy (2008)

Come, Let Us Adore Him

A Daily Advent Devotional

Paul David Tripp

WHEATON, ILLINOIS

Come, Let Us Adore Him: A Daily Advent Devotional

Published by Crossway
1300 Crescent Street
Wheaton, Illinois 60187

Lyrics from the following hymns are cited in the December 4 and 23 devotions: "Hark, the Herald Angels Sing," by Charles Wesley, 1739; "Joy to the World," by Isaac Watts, 1719; "Silent Night," by Joseph Mohr, 1818.

Lyrics from the following hymns are cited in the December 23 devotion: "O Come, All Ye Faithful," by John Francis Wade, 1751; "O Come, O Come Emmanuel," trans. John Mason Neale, 1851; "Thou Didst Leave Thy Throne," by E. S. Elliot, 1864.

Cover design: Tyler Deeb, Misc. Goods Co.

First printing 2017

Printed in China

Hardcover ISBN: 978-1-4335-5669-2
ePub ISBN: 978-1-4335-5672-2
PDF ISBN: 978-1-4335-5670-8
Mobipocket ISBN: 978-1-4335-5671-5

Library of Congress Cataloging-in-Publication Data

Names: Tripp, Paul David, 1950– author.
Title: Come, let us adore Him : a daily Advent devotional / Paul David Tripp.
Description: Wheaton : Crossway, 2017. | Includes index.
Identifiers: LCCN 2016056320 (print) | LCCN 2017026411 (ebook) | ISBN 9781433556708 (pdf) | ISBN 9781433556715 (mobi) | ISBN 9781433556722 (epub) | ISBN 9781433556692 (hc)
Subjects: LCSH: Advent—Meditations. | Christmas—Meditations.
Classification: LCC BV40 (ebook) | LCC BV40 .T75 2017 (print) | DDC 242/.332—dc23
LC record available at https://lccn.loc.gov/2016056320

Crossway is a publishing ministry of Good News Publishers.

RRD 27 26 25 24 23 22 21 20 19 18 17
15 14 13 12 11 10 9 8 7 6 5 4 3 2 1

My mind is a puzzle, each piece placed by a pastor, professor, or mentor greater than I, all working under the gracious guiding hand of God. Through them I have come to know the Word, learned to interpret life, been humbled by a sense of my own need, and grown to love my rescuing Savior. To all those willing instruments in my past and present and by God's grace in my future, I say, "Thank you."

Introduction

It is a mind-boggling, hard-to-grasp, awesome story unlike any other story ever told. But what makes this story so wonderful and so important is not that its plot is way beyond anything you would've ever conceived. What makes this story vital to know and understand is that it is not a well-crafted fantasy. The thing that should make you stop in your tracks, activate your heart and mind, and fall to your knees is that this story is *real*. It took place in real time at real locations with real people. All human history was marching to the specific point in time when this story would unfold, and the implications of the events of this story reach to everyone who has lived since. The Christmas story is the story of stories.

When writing this devotional, I was brought to a new place of wonder and worship as I considered that that baby boy in the manger was not only a real human baby but also fully God. For the months it took to write this collection of meditations, it was wonderful to consider day after day that God knew that the only way to fix everything sin had broken was to give us the ultimate gift, the gift of himself. My prayer is that focusing on the glory of the incarnation of Jesus will fill you with wonder too.

Permit me to share what motivated me to write a Christmas devotional. I've thought a lot about the danger of familiarity in our lives as the children of God. It is good to be familiar with the story of the gospel of Jesus Christ. It means that God has met you by grace. It means that he has opened the eyes of your heart to what, without him, you would not see or understand. He has drawn you close to his side. He has pulled back the curtain and shown you the deep mysteries of his redeeming plan. He has blessed you with the presence of his Spirit, who continues to illumine his truth for you. You are familiar with the story of the gospel of Jesus Christ because the love of God has been lavished on you.

But familiarity often does bad things to us. Often when we become familiar with things, we begin to take them for granted. When we are familiar with things, we tend to quit examining them. Often when we are familiar with things, we quit noticing them. When we are familiar with things, we tend not to celebrate them as we once did. Familiarity tends to rob us of our wonder. And here's what's important about this: what has captured the wonder of our hearts will control the way we live.

Let me give you an example. Pretend that you have moved to a new neighborhood and the first morning, when you go out to walk your dog, you happen upon a beautiful municipal rose garden. Although Fido is yanking on his leash, you just stand there, blown away at the display of early-morning beauty that is before you. You can't wait to get home to tell your family what you discovered, and you're excited about taking them there to see it too. But as you walk by that garden day after day, something happens to you. Within a few weeks you walk by without stopping, and in a few months you don't even notice the roses anymore. Familiarity has done this to you; what you once celebrated, you now don't even notice.

Sadly, many of us aren't gripped by the stunningly magnificent events and truths of the birth of Jesus anymore. Sadly, many of us are no longer gripped by wonder as we consider what this story tells us about the character and plan of God. Sadly, many of us are no longer humbled by what the incarnation of Jesus tells us about ourselves. We walk by the garden of the incarnation, but we don't see the roses of grace anymore. Our eyes have gone lazy and our hearts have grown cold.

I know how easy it is for me, on any given day, to forget who I am and what I have been given in the person and work of Jesus. Other things in life capture my attention and the allegiance of my heart. Other things rise to levels of importance in my mind, way beyond their true importance. And when other things capture and control my heart, little room remains for wonder and worship. Familiarity often means that what is very important may no longer exercise important influence over us in the way it should.

So I wrote this devotional with the prayer that God would use it to recapture your attention. I wrote it with hope that this amazing story would reactivate your awe. I hope that as you read, your heart will be surprised by things in this story you've never seen before or maybe haven't seen in a very long time. I am going to ask you to come with me, kneel down, and look into that manger. I will ask you to look up and listen carefully to the song of the angels. I'm going to ask you to examine the wonder of the shepherds. And I will help you to grasp how this story is meant to enliven, motivate, excite, and transform you.

One year, for the thirty-one days of December, I decided I would dedicate the three tweets that I post every morning to the Christmas story. Those tweets are the foundation of the meditations that make up this devotional. Each meditation begins with a tweet, which is then explained, defined, expanded, and applied in the meditation that follows. Following each meditation are Scriptures to use for further study.

A Word to Parents

I added something in this devotional that wasn't in *New Morning Mercies* (Crossway 2014). At the end of each meditation I present *one central theme*, one core truth from the narrative of Jesus's birth for you to discuss with your children. Obviously, these meditations were written to adults, but they have nuggets of truth that every child could and should grasp. You can approach this devotional in several ways with your children. You may want to select a portion of the meditation to read to them, and then discuss the one central theme. You may think the meditation is too deep for them and choose to read all or a portion of the support Scripture, and then talk with them about the core truth. You may just want to talk to them about the core truth.

In a culture that uses this season to get children to dream about how their lives would be made better by possessing a certain material thing, where Christmas has been reduced to a shopper's nightmare and a retailer's dream, it is vital to draw the wonder of our children away from the next great toy and toward the wonder of the coming of our great Lord and Savior, Jesus. Use these devotionals with the hope that, as you do, God will plant seeds of true faith in their young hearts. Take a few moments every morning or at the dinner table to take the thoughts of your children away from trees, carols, toys, snowballs, and cookies. Invest the time needed to introduce them to the multifaceted glory of the grace that is displayed in the coming of the promised Messiah to earth. You can use this devotional to fight what familiarity has already done to the way their young hearts think about Christmas.

May the glory of the best gift ever recapture our hearts so that we really do come to adore him and so that we will all live with a renewed appreciation for the grace that we have found in him.

May your Christmas be rich in spiritual blessings!

December 1

The angels sang because the everlasting Father had come to extend arms of redeeming grace to all who would give their hearts to him.

It is a wonderful, mysterious, hard-to-grasp, and beyond-the-scope-of-our-normal-reasoning story. But when you get it, when you come to fully understand the purpose and implications of this story, you will sing too. This story's amazing plot wasn't written when Mary got pregnant or when prophets began foretelling it or when God announced it after the disastrous rebellion of Adam and Eve. This story is so miraculous in every way that it could have only come out of the mind of God in eternity before the foundations of the earth were laid down by his mighty hand. It points to the divine imagination and screams the power of the divine hand. No man could write this plot and if he did, no man could expedite what he had written. This story is itself an argument for the existence of God and is a portrait of his holy character.

The beautiful world that God had created was now broken and groaning—the direct result of the rebellion of the ones God had made in his own image and had placed his guiding and providing love upon. The evidence of its brokenness was everywhere, from the inner recesses of the hearts of people, to violence and corruption of government, to the existence of plagues and diseases. Sure, there was beauty still to be seen, but the whole world groaned under the weight of its brokenness. It would have been just for God to stay his distance, to let the world quake and groan. It would have been a just response to the arrogant rebellion that brought this brokenness on the world. But in one of the gorgeous mysteries of God's sovereign grace, he looked on his broken, rebellious world with eyes of mercy.

Yes, God would act decisively, and his actions would be what he had planned in the beginning, but they would be a stunning surprise to every mere mortal. His response would not be condemnation and judgment. His response would not be a meting out of justice. Rather, his response would be intervention and rescue. He would do in grace what the law could never do. He would do in grace what we could never do for ourselves. He would do what philosophers could never conceive, what leaders could never strategize, and what poets could never imagine. He would offer the only thing that would ever address the need and solve the problem. He, himself, would become the greatest, most costly, most transformational gift ever.

God would take on human flesh and invade his sin-broken world with his wisdom, power, glory, and grace. But he wouldn't descend to a palace. Instead, the Lord Almighty, the Creator, the sovereign King over all things would humble himself and take on the form of servant; he would live on our behalf the life we could have never lived, he would willingly die the death that you and I deserve to die, and he would rise from his tomb as the conqueror of sin and death. He would suffer every single day of his life so that he could, with his life, give grace to rebels, extend love to those who would deny his existence, impart wisdom to those who think they know better, and extend forgiveness to everyone who seeks him. His coming stands as an affirmation that he will not relent, he will not be satisfied until sin and suffering are no more and we are like him, dwelling with him in unity, peace, and harmony forever and ever.

It is true that you just can't write this stuff! The majesty of the patient and forgiving love of this story defies words. The implications of this birth are not only transformational to the cosmos, but also eternal in their extent. This is the story of Jesus, born in a barn in Bethlehem. The Messiah the earth cried for now cries to be held by Mary and will soon cry in torment of the cross of salvation. He came to suffer because he came to save. The angels sang because finally hope had come. Don't you want to join them?

For further study: Luke 2:13–14; Revelation 5:8–11

For parents and children:

Central theme: Singing

Ask you children what their favorite song is, ask them why they think people sing, read Luke 2:13–14 to them, and talk about why the angels sang at the birth of Jesus.

December 2

Jesus knew he had come not just to preach the gospel of sacrifice, but also to be that sacrifice, yet he was perfectly willing.

One of the dark character qualities of sin that we don't recognize as much as we should is unwillingness. We're often unwilling to do what God says if it doesn't make sense to us. We're often unwilling to inconvenience ourselves for the needs of someone else. We're regularly unwilling to wait. We're often unwilling to be open and honest. We're too often unwilling to consider the loving rebuke of another. We struggle to be willing to say no to our own wrong thoughts and desires. We often struggle to be willing to answer God's ministry call. Often we are unwilling to admit that we are wrong. Too often we struggle to serve willingly and to give generously. Unwillingness is one of sin's powerful damaging results.

So here's what the Christmas story is all about: a willing Savior is born to rescue unwilling people from themselves because there is no other way. Jesus was willing to leave the splendor of eternity to come to this broken and groaning world. He was willing to take on human flesh with all its frailty. He was willing to endure an ignominious birth in a stable. He was willing to go through the dependency of childhood. He was willing to expose himself to all the hardships of life in this fallen world. He was willing to submit to his own law. He was willing to do his Father's will at every point. He was willing to serve, when he deserved to be served. He was willing to be misunderstood and mistreated. He was willing to endure rejection and gross injustice. He was willing to preach a message that would cause him personal harm. He was willing to suffer public mockery. He was willing to endure physical torture. He was willing to go through the pain of his Father's rejection. He was willing to die. He was willing to rise and ascend to be our constant advocate. Jesus was willing.

You see, it's not just the Christmas story; rather, the entire redemptive story hinges on one thing—the eternal willingness of Jesus. Without his willingness, you and I would be without hope and without God. Without his willingness, we would be left with the power and curse of sin. Without his willingness, we would be eternally damned. During this season of celebrating don't forget to stop and celebrate your Savior's willingness. His willingness is your hope in life, death, and eternity.

But there is even more to be said. The Advent willingness of Jesus is your guarantee that he continues to be willing today. Right here, right now, he is willing to love you on your very worst day. Right now he is willing to forgive you again and again. Here and now he is willing to be patient as you continue to grow and mature. Right now he is willing to battle on your behalf against evil within and without. Here and now he is willing to teach you through his Word. Now he is willing to supply every one of your spiritual needs. Now he is willing to be faithful even when you're not. He, right now, is willing to empower you when you're weak and to restore you when you've fallen. He is willing to comfort you when you are discouraged and protect you when you've stepped into danger. And he remains willing to do everything necessary to feed, guide, sustain, and protect you until eternity is your final home.

You see, the Advent story reminds us that our past, present, and future hope rest not on our willingness, but on the willingness of the One for whom the angels sang, the shepherds worshiped, and the magi searched. Willing Jesus is the only hope for unwilling sinners!

For further study: Hebrews 12:1–3

For parents and children:
Central theme: Willingness
Talk to your children about what it means to be willing and how the sin in our hearts makes us unwilling. Encourage them to talk about places in their lives where they're unwilling. Then talk about how Jesus came to earth and willingly did hard things because he loves us.

December 3

All the promises of the prophets were carried on the shoulders of the One born in Bethlehem, and he fulfilled them all.

Maybe you've endured one of those awkward moments when important visitors, friends you haven't seen for a while, or distant relatives show up unannounced. You're glad they're there, but you're also kind of mad because they didn't let you know they were coming. It's good to see them, but you would've enjoyed the luxury of being prepared for their coming. Most of us don't like being surprised by someone significant showing up unannounced.

Well, Jesus didn't show up on earth unannounced. A whole company of prophets spoke a myriad of prophecies that not only pointed to the surety of his coming, but also made specific promises about what his coming would produce.

Micah prophesied that Jesus would be *born in Bethlehem*. "But you, O Bethlehem Ephrathah, who are too little to be among the clans of Judah, from you shall come forth for me one who is to be ruler in Israel, whose coming forth is from of old, from ancient days" (Mic. 5:2).

Isaiah prophesied something that was both very specific and unthinkable, that Jesus would be *born of a virgin.* "Therefore the Lord himself will give you a sign. Behold, the virgin shall conceive and bear a son, and shall call his name Immanuel" (Isa. 7:14).

Genesis 22:18 tells us that Jesus would *be born as a descendant of Abraham* and as such would be the ultimate fulfillment of God's covenant promises: "And in your offspring shall all the nations of the earth be blessed" (see Num. 24:17).

The Old Testament also foretells that Jesus would *be called out of Egypt*: "When Israel was a child, I loved him, and out of Egypt I called my son" (Hos. 11:1; see Matt. 2:13).

Jeremiah tells us that Jesus would be born in the *middle of the worst kind of human suffering*: "A voice is heard in Ramah, lamentation and bitter weeping. Rachel is weeping for her children; she refuses to be comforted for her children, because they are no more" (Jer. 31:15; see Matt. 2:16–18).

These prophecies remind us that the coming of Jesus is the result of the unstoppable zeal of a God of glorious redeeming grace. God wouldn't leave his world in its evil-scarred condition of brokenness. He was unwilling to leave us lost in our sin and in hopeless bondage to the rebellion of our own evil hearts. He wouldn't let his story end with dark moral failure and the requisite divine judgment. These, and many other prophecies, remind us that the great author of history's plot determined that the overarching theme of his story would not be judgment, but grace. And he knew that if the story were to be a grace story, the central character would have to be none other than his Son. Only the divine Son of God would be up to the task of living a perfectly righteous life in the middle of sin and suffering, dying an acceptable death that would satisfy his Father's holy requirements, and rising out of the tomb of his death as the author of eternal life for all who place their trust in him.

But here's what you need to understand today. The surety of these past prophecies and the specificity of how Jesus fulfilled them is also your guaranteed future hope. The story that the prophets of old pointed to has not yet come to its final conclusion. This means that today, in your life and mine, God is still working his unstoppable plot, and he will not relent or rest until all that the prophets predicted is fully realized in the lives of every one of his children.

Know today that it's not just you who battles with sin and struggles in the middle of suffering. The Messiah, prophesied by those saints of old, battles on your behalf, and he will not quit until sin and suffering are no more. Like movie trailers, the prophets give you a taste of God's plot, of which you now live in the middle. The movement of the plot doesn't rest on your wisdom, power, or goodness, but on the unstoppable zeal of the One who is perfect in his holiness and plenteous in his grace, and because it does, the last chapter, for which we all long, is secure.

For further study: Micah 5:1–6

For parents and children:

Central theme: Promises

Ask your children what a promise is and get them to think about why we make promises. Talk to them about how the birth of Jesus proves to us that God always keeps the promises he makes.

December 4

The angels sang a glory song because Glory had come to earth to unleash his glory on all who would put their trust in him.

I love Christmas. I love the excitement of the season, the gift giving, Christmas cookies, decorating the biggest tree we can get in our home, the special moments with people whom I love, but most of all the deep, encouraging, humbling, and hope-giving story that is at the heart of this season. I can remember as a little boy the excitement that would begin to grow as my mom and my grandma began making dozens and dozens of cookies. And I remember how my excitement would elevate as my dad began to drag out the Christmas decorations. But maybe the thing I loved the most was the music. Sure, I liked hearing all those silly seasonal songs as we went shopping in downtown Toledo, but what I loved then and love even more now are those rich hymns about the birth of Jesus. I learned them as a boy, but I understand them today, line by line, in a way I never did during all the excitement of those boyhood Christmases.

There is something particularly glorious about the hymns that explain and define the significance of the incarnation of Jesus Christ. Words like "Veiled in flesh the Godhead see; hail the incarnate Deity" or "He comes to make his blessing flow far as the curse is found" or "Radiant beams from thy holy face, with the dawn of redeeming grace" shimmer with glory. This makes sense because they echo the glory song that the angels first sang on the night when the most glorious thing in history happened: God took on human form. Let these words ring in your heart for a moment: God took on human form. God became a man. Deity took on humanity. Glory came to earth in common human form. If you or I had been writing the big redemptive story, we would have never conceived something so amazing and miraculous as God actually coming on a rescue mission as a real human person. There is only one word that captures this one amazing, history-altering event: *glory*.

The angels sang a glory song not only because the events about which they sang were glorious, but also because the One who came was, is, and will ever be the sum and definition of glory. The angels sang of glory because Glory had come to earth to rescue us from the inglory of sin and to unleash the forgiving and transforming glory of his grace on all who would believe. The hymn of the angels, and the hymns that have been written by God's people since, shimmer with glory because the incarnation of Jesus is about a glorious Savior coming to give glorious grace to people who have forsaken his glory for the temporarily satisfying shadow glories of the created world. If you write a hymn about glory, you will end up penning glorious things.

But there's something else I want us to think about. The angels, as they sang their glory song that night, began the singing of a glory song that would never end. God's people have penned and sung glory songs about Jesus ever since. Whenever and wherever they gather, they sing together of the birth, the life, the death, the resurrection, the promises, the presence, the power, and the grace of Jesus. Around the world hearts lift and hope comes rushing in as melodies carry the precious truths of God's most wonderful gift to us, the gift of his Son.

And think about this: the final book of the Bible, Revelation, invites us to listen to the voices of those who have passed over to their final and eternal home. What do we hear them doing? We hear them singing glory songs about Jesus, just as the angels did on the night of his birth. "Hallelujah! Salvation and glory and power belong to our God" (Rev. 19:1); "Hallelujah! For the Lord our God the Almighty reigns. Let us rejoice and exult and give him the glory" (Rev. 19:6–7). On into eternity the song echoes. It is the celebration chant of the redeemed. And one day we will join that multitude, no longer looking forward in hope but looking back with the security of redemption accomplished, and with the angels and the saints of old we too will sing glory songs about Jesus forever and ever and ever. Yes, it is true: that night the angels began a song that will never ever end. The Savior who rescued your heart now claims your song. Have you joined the choir?

For further study: Revelation 19:1–10

For parents and children:
Central theme: Glory
Get your children to talk about what they think *glory* means. Ask them if there are any glorious things in their lives. Help them to understand that every glorious created thing is meant to point them to the glory of God. Then help them to see that there is nothing more glorious than the coming of God to earth to do for us what we could never do for ourselves.

December 5

The incarnation of Jesus Christ pointedly preaches our inescapable need for radical, personal, and moral rescue and forgiveness.

One of the primary purposes of the incarnation of Jesus is to humble each and every one of us. Let me say it this way: only when you accept the very, very bad news of Jesus's birth will you then be excited about its very, very good news. Good news is only ever good news to people who know that they need good news. Ten dollars is extremely good news to a poor man, but would not even get noticed by a rich man. The promise of healing is wonderfully good news to a very sick woman, but would not even get the attention of a woman who was in good health. Jesus's birth is both the worst and the best news ever, and understanding both will change your life forever.

It is humbling to accept that God came, in the person of Jesus, to live the way that we were created to live, but would never live, to die the death that each one of us deserves to die, and to rise out of the tomb, defeating sin and death because there was simply no other way. God knew that our condition was so desperately grave that he was willing to go to this extent to reach and rescue us. Ponder the fact that God was willing to control the events of world history to bring this world to the place where conditions were right for Jesus to come, simply because we had no power whatsoever to help ourselves out of our desperate state. Humanity was so incredibly messed up that there was only one solution for us: God himself!

God knew that something lurks inside all of us that twists every thought, that diverts every desire, that shapes the direction of every choice, and that controls every word and action. And he knew that because this thing was inside us and not outside us, we would never be able to conquer it on our own. For all the beauty of his law, he knew the law could expose us, it could guide us, and it could indict us, but it would never be able to rescue us. So the only hope for messed up and desperate people like us was the sending of the ultimate rescuer, his Son, the Lord Jesus Christ.

The reason the birth of Jesus is such gloriously wonderful news is that in his birth God offers you and me the only solution to the fundamental brokenness of sin that is the core tragedy of every one of our lives. So confessing our brokenness is the only way we will ever fully understand and celebrate the birth of the Messiah, Jesus.

Let me define the brokenness of sin, which every human being shares, with five words: *separation, inability, delusion, judgment, hopelessness*. First, because of sin we exist in a from-birth state of *separation* from God, for whose glory we were created and in whose fellowship we were meant to live. Separation from God robs us of the core reason for our existence. Sin also renders us *unable*. It makes it impossible for us to think as we were made to think, to desire what we were created to desire, to speak as we were designed to speak, and to behave as God intended us to behave. How sad is it to be a human being, but not be able to live as you were created to live! Because sin blinds, it also leaves us in a constant state of *delusion*. We think we know ourselves well, but we don't. We assess that we are more righteous than we actually are, and because we do, we don't seek the help that we desperately need.

But on top of these disasters is something even more terrible. Sin doesn't just leave us separate from God; it places us under his *judgment*. Because we have rebelled against him and demanded our own way, we have again and again broken his law. How tragic is it to be under the judgment of the One for whom you were created! Yet there is one more thing to be said about the effect of sin. Sin leaves us *hopeless*. Since sin is a matter of the heart, a condition of our nature, it is impossible for us to escape it on our own. We are under its destructive effects and power, yet we can do nothing to help ourselves. The apostle Paul describes our lives apart from the amazing grace of the birth of Jesus as "having no hope and without God in the world" (Eph. 2:12).

The beautiful news of the Christmas season is that God wasn't willing to leave us in this tragic and desperate state. He had every right to make his final response to us be one of judgment, but he wasn't willing. He chose to respond another way, not because of what he saw in us, but because of what was in him. At Christmas we celebrate a God who is glorious in his abundant love and patient mercy. He chose to give grace to those who could never deserve his favor. He chose to rescue those who could not help themselves. He chose to forgive those who had rebelled again and again. He chose to not leave us in our blindness, but to open our eyes. He chose to empower the unable. And because he chose all of these things, he chose to send his Son. The glory of the birth of Jesus becomes even more glorious when it is seen through the humbling lens of the desperate condition that was the reason for his coming. Accept the very bad news of Christmas today, so that you can celebrate even more joyfully its wonderfully good news.

For further study: Ephesians 2:1–10

For parents and children:
Central theme: Broken
Ask your children what we mean when we say something is broken. Ask them if there are any broken things in their lives. Get them to talk about what they think it means when the Bible says that sin has left all of us broken. Then talk to them about the fact that Jesus came because we are broken and we cannot fix ourselves.

December 6

That baby in the manger came as our ultimate substitute. Everything he would do, he would do on our behalf, for our salvation.

For once I was excited to go to Spanish class. Word had gotten out that our regular Spanish teacher was sick, and we would have a substitute. I had also heard something about the substitute: she wasn't a Spanish teacher. I thought I had hit the jackpot. We would probably do nothing in class and would surely be assigned no homework. For the first time in my life, I rushed to Spanish class.

My apologies to any substitutes who may read this, but I grew up expecting very little from the substitute teachers who filled in for our regular instructors. They tended to be unprepared (probably because they were called at the last minute) and not very knowledgeable (probably because they were filling outside of their area of expertise), and because of these things, they were often nervous and ill at ease.

The Bible clearly teaches that Jesus came as our substitute, but in hearing that, you can throw out all experiences you have had with substitute teachers. Jesus came as the ultimate substitute to stand in our place, but he came to live infinitely better than any of us could ever live on our own. One of the ways the Bible talks about this is to call Jesus the "second Adam." It is a provocative title, worth examining.

The first Adam was created by God and placed in a perfect world, in perfect relationship with God. Adam literally had it all: no earthly needs unmet and no separation between him and God. But in an act of outrageous rebellion against God, he took his life into his own hands, stepped outside God's boundaries, and did exactly what God had warned him not to do. He had it all, but he miserably failed, and when he did, sin, sickness, and suffering entered the world. Like fine china thrown on the pavement, the perfection of the world shattered. Adam now lived under God's judgment, and the world groaned in brokenness.

What the world cried out for was a substitute, but not any substitute would do. This substitute needed to be special in every way, so that he would not fail the test as the first Adam had. He had to be perfect in righteousness and mighty in power, or he too would fail. No one on earth could meet the requirements, so God sent the only One who was up to the task, the only One who would not succumb to the pressure and fail the test. God sent the one person whom he knew was qualified to be the second Adam: his Son.

Everything Jesus did, from the first moment of his birth

until his ascension to the right hand of his Father, he did as our substitute. What he did in every situation, location, and relationship, he did in our place. Every decision he made, every temptation he faced, every trial or moment of suffering he endured, was on our behalf. But this is vital to understand: he never failed one single test. He faced all the ravages of life in this fallen world without sinning in any way. He was the perfect substitute.

And because Jesus was the perfect substitute, on the cross he made the perfectly acceptable sacrifice, and because he did, he satisfied God's requirement, and the penalty for our sin was lifted. Jesus, the second Adam, is our first and only hope in life and death. Because of his substitution we are redeemed. God sent One in our place who would do infinitely better than we could ever do, because our salvation depended upon it. The Christmas story is the most glorious stand-in story ever!

For further study: 2 Corinthians 5:17–21

For parents and children:
Central theme: Substitute
Ask you children what they think a substitute is. Talk about substitute teachers and substitutes in sports. Talk about how usually substitutes are not as qualified as the people they're working in the place of. Then talk about how Jesus was born to be our substitute, to do things for us that we could never do on our own.

December 7

God sent his Son to provide rescue and forgiveness for those who had ignored his existence and rebelled against his rule. That's grace!

If you had to summarize the Christmas story with one word, what word would you choose? Now, your word would have to capture what this story points to as the core of human need and the way God would meet that need. Do you have a word in mind? Maybe you're thinking that it's just not possible to summarize the greatest story ever with one word. But I think you can. Let's consider one lovely, amazing, history-changing, and eternally significant word.

It doesn't take paragraph after paragraph, written on page after page, filling volume after volume to communicate how God chose to respond to the outrageous rebellion of Adam and Eve and the subtle and not-so-subtle rebellion of everyone since. God's response to the sin of people against his rightful and holy rule can be captured in a single word. I wonder if you thought, "I know the word: *grace*." But the single word that captures God's response to sin even better than the word *grace* is not a theological word; it is a name. That name is Jesus.

God's response wasn't a thing. It wasn't the establishment of an institution. It wasn't a process of intervention. It wasn't some new divine program. In his infinite wisdom God knew that the only thing that could rescue us from ourselves and repair the horrendous damage that sin had done to the world was not a thing at all. It was a person, his Son, the Lord Jesus.

God's response to our rebellion was to give us himself. He is the great redeeming, transforming gift. He is the rescue. He is the forgiveness. He is the restoration. He is life, hope, peace, and security. There is no salvation apart from him. There is no deliverance from the presence and power of sin apart from him. There is no restored relationship with God apart from him. There is no new heaven and new earth apart from him. There is no end to sickness and suffering apart from him. There is no defeat of death apart from him. There simply is no such thing as redeeming grace and all that it means apart from the willingness of God to give us himself in the person of the Messiah, Jesus.

Jesus *is* the grace of God, given to sinners who cannot free themselves from the death grip of sin. Look into that manger at that baby boy and see grace. The Christmas story is about grace in its most shocking and surprising form. The Lord of lords, one of incalculable glory, humbles himself and takes on human flesh and blood. The Creator, in a way that boggles the mind, becomes the created. The One who made a perfect world now exposes himself to a world stained with imperfections. The judge of all things places himself under judgment. The One who deserves worship becomes the Lamb of sacrifice. The One who deserves everyone's love subjects himself to being despised and rejected. The One who owns all things lives with no place to call home and no place to rest his weary head.

Here in one single word, the name Jesus, is the shocking turn in the redemptive story. In sovereignty and with power, God would respond to the sorry condition of his world. With holy authority, he would deal with the image bearers who had turned their backs on him. Yet he would deal with the ravages of sin not with the tools of judgment, but with a single tool of grace, Jesus. You simply cannot use the word *grace* without connecting that word to Jesus. Yes, it needs to be said again and again and again. Jesus *is* the grace of God to sinners. Without his life, death, and resurrection, grace would be a sentiment devoid of any helpfulness. Without the gift of Jesus, grace would be a promise with no power. Without the presence, life, and work of that baby in the manger, there is no light at the end of the tunnel for sinners. There is no happy ending for rebels. There is no home waiting for the lost. There is only darkness, defeat, judgment, and death.

This season, in the midst of all the celebrations and gift-giving, be careful to remember that at the center of what we celebrate is one game-changing, life-altering, hope-giving reality: grace is a person, and his name is Jesus. God knew that nothing else would ever repair what sin had broken, so he gave us the ultimate gift of gifts, the gift of his Son. It's not enough to say that Jesus came to preach grace to us. It is not enough to say that he came to give grace to us. No, Jesus *is* God's redeeming grace, given to those who without him would have no hope in life or in death. Now that's worth celebrating, not just on one special day but on every day of your life, and for the rest of eternity too!

For further study: Hebrews 1:1–4

For parents and children:
Central theme: Jesus
Talk to your children about how you get out tools whenever something is broken. Then help them to understand that God knew that the only way to fix all the things sin had broken was not with a tool, but with a person. That's why God sent his Son, Jesus, to earth to be born in that manger in Bethlehem.

December 8

The shepherds came to worship the Prince of Peace, who came to finally bridge the separation between God and mankind and purchase peace.

We've all had weird, awkward moments with others. You probably hate those moments as much as I do. You say something but it doesn't come out right, and what comes out is embarrassing. Your embarrassing little quip is then followed by what is probably a few seconds, but seems like an eternity of strained silence. You then feel the need to explain, but you just end up digging a deeper hole for yourself. You wish one of your listeners would rise to your rescue, but no one does. Finally something else happens that grabs everybody's attention, and the horribly awkward moment ends. But it doesn't really end for you; you carry it with you for the rest of the night. In fact, it is the pain of the moment that wakes you up the next morning. A few years later, that awkward moment has morphed into a humorous moment, and you retell the story over and over again to the delight and amusement of your friends.

I want you to think today about the most horribly awkward moment in human history. This one wasn't a minor moment of embarrassment, and it will never morph into a humorous story. As you read the account, you know you are dealing with something so shocking and out of place that the world will never be the same again. Every time I read this account, I want to weep. Every time I think about it, I am hit with the painful thought that it really did happen and that we still see its results in our lives today. When you read it, you better know that this is not the way things were meant to be, or you will never understand the biblical story, and Christmas will never make the kind of sense that it should make to you.

Here is the Bible's account:

> And they heard the sound of the Lord God walking in the garden in the cool of the day, and the man and his wife hid themselves from the presence of the Lord God among the trees of the garden. But the Lord God called to the man and said to him, "Where are you?" And he said, "I heard the sound of you in the garden, and I was afraid, because I was naked, and I hid myself." He said, "Who told you that you were naked? Have you eaten of the tree of which I commanded you not to eat?" The man said, "The woman whom you gave to be with me, she gave me fruit of the tree, and I ate." Then the Lord God said to the woman, "What is this that you have done?" The woman said, "The serpent deceived me, and I ate." (Gen. 3:8–13)

Adam and Eve had just endured the first awkward, embarrassing, shame-inducing moment between them. For the first time they realized that they were without clothing, and they felt instant shame. This is an immediate clue that their disobedience had destroyed their innocence, and human relationships would never be the same again. But that sad and shameful moment pales in comparison to what happened next. God was walking through the garden, and rather than being filled with awe and joy at the thought of his presence, Adam and Eve were filled with fear. Their reaction was weird, awkward, and unusual. They had been designed for intimate, moment-by-moment, loving, and worshipful communion with him. They were made to delight in God and he in them. They were created to live in an unbreakable bond of love with him. So their reaction seems strange and out of place. It tells us that something has gone drastically wrong.

God notices that they have not approached him with the usual expectant joy, and so he calls out to them, inquiring where they are. Adam answers and confesses that he was naked and afraid. The effects of sin are immediate and catastrophic. The bond between God and mankind has been broken. Fear has replaced love. Hiding has replaced communion. Adam and Eve have not only damaged their spirituality, but have lost a huge chunk of their humanity. It is a tragedy of historic and universal proportion. Made to live in the center of God's love, people hide from him. In the psyche of every human being since lives this weird and uncomfortable battle between hunger for God and a desire to hide from him.

Sin has broken the most important relationship in all of life, the relationship between people and their Creator. This separation alters everything in each of our lives. That's why it is so wonderful and encouraging to know that Jesus came to earth to be the Prince of Peace. Through his life, death, and resurrection, he would make peace between God and us. By his righteous life, he would earn our acceptance with God and purchase our right to be God's children. It is this vertical peace that then allows us to live in peace and harmony with one another. The fearful awkwardness between us and God has been forever broken by Jesus, so we can run with confidence into God's presence and know that he will never turn us away.

For further study: Ephesians 2:11–22

For parents and children:
Central theme: Peace
Get your children to talk about what they think peace is. Ask them what it would mean in your family if everyone lived in peace together. Help them to understand that sin means we no longer live in peace with God, and that Jesus came to live and die so that we could enjoy peace with God now and forever.

December 9

Jesus left his lofty place to rescue glory thieves who insert themselves into his place and make it all about them.

In 2 Corinthians 5:15, Paul is quite clear about the reason for the birth, life, death, and resurrection of Jesus. He says, "And he died for all, that those who live might no longer live for themselves but for him who for their sake died and was raised." No human being has ever successfully escaped the draw of sin that Paul points to here. Sin draws us away from God's glory toward our glory. Sin pulls us away from God's kingdom and produces in us an obsessive allegiance to our little kingdom of one. Sin makes us less concerned about what God wants and more concerned about what we want. Sin causes us to be more excited about our personal plans than we are about the things that God has planned for us. Sin makes us more focused on our feelings than we are about God's will.

Here's what sin does. It causes each of us to place ourselves in the center of our worlds and make life all about us. So we always feel the need to be in control. We hate it if we're not healthy. We want to be affluent and surrounded by beautiful possessions. We can't cope if we're not surrounded by people who like and respect us. We want life to be predictable and easy. We don't want obstacles in our way or suffering of any kind in our path. So because we can't control any of these things, we're perennially unhappy with life, and sadly, often with God.

You see, our problem is not just that we live in a broken world and that its brokenness enters our doors; beneath that reality is a much deeper problem. We have a glory problem. We have preferred living for ourselves over living for something and someone bigger than ourselves. In our marriages, in our parenting, in our work, in our friendships, and in the church, we have made life all about us. We have tended to reduce the active field of our concern down to the tiny confines of our wants, our needs, our plans, our satisfaction, and our happiness. It's not wrong to want some control, or to want to be right, or to like beautiful possessions, or to be surrounded by a community of love, but it's wrong and spiritually dangerous for those things to rule your heart.

Let me give you an example by asking a rather intrusive question. How much of your anger in the last two months had anything whatsoever to do with God's call, his kingdom, and his glory? You see, if we're honest, we're not angry because the people around us are breaking God's law; we are angry because they're breaking *our* law. They get in the way of what we want or what we think we need. Perhaps, at street level, we're not living for the glory of God at all. Perhaps in ways we're not conscious of, we have shrunk life down to the size of our own glory. Maybe it really is true that somehow, someway, sin makes us all glory thieves. We steal for ourselves what belongs to God. We put ourselves in God's place. Perhaps life really is one big unending glory battle. It's because we would never, ever win this battle on our own that Jesus came.

This is where we are confronted and comforted by the glorious goodness of God and the radical humility of Jesus. Our God of infinite glory looked on glory thieves not with jealous derision but with redeeming love. And because he did, he commissioned his Son to leave his rightful glory position to become a servant even to death, so that you and I could be liberated from the prison of self-glory that is the doom of every sinner. Not only that, but the saving work of Jesus unleashes God's glory onto us. As his children we are showered with the glory of his forgiveness, the glory of his love, the glory of his wisdom, the glory of his power, the glory of his mercy, the glory of his sovereign rule, the glory of his promises, and the glory of his presence. And the showering of glory on us progressively turns our hearts away from our individualistic commitment to our own glory to once again live for the thing for which we were created: the glory of God.

Here is the movement of the Christmas story: glory forsaken (Jesus), glory liberated (our self-glory), glory restored (our living for the glory of God). The Son of Glory came to fight our glory battle so that we would be freed from our bondage to any other glory but the glory of God. May your celebration today be bigger and deeper than awesome Christmas decorations, wonderful Christmas food, and cool Christmas gifts. May you glory in the real glory of this season. May you celebrate your glory-liberation while you recognize your need for further freedom, and may you remember your Savior. His humiliation is your liberation. And may you always be blown away by the stunning catalog of glories that have been showered down on you because of the amazing goodness of God and the humble willingness of Jesus.

For further study: Philippians 3:12–20

For parents and children:
Central theme: Thieves
Ask you children what they would do if someone stole something very valuable from them. Ask them if they ever took something that didn't belong to them. Then help them to understand that we're all thieves because there is something very valuable that we all steal from God—his glory. Then help them to understand that Jesus was born not to condemn thieves but to forgive them.

December 10

The Way, the Truth, and the Life was in the manger, causing angels to rejoice, Mary to wonder, shepherds to worship, and us to have hope.

The Christmas story clearly shows that the hope of the universe is a person. Hope was what the angels sang about. Hope lay in the manger. Hope caused Mary to wonder in her heart. It was hope the shepherds came to worship. Hope was presented with gifts from the Magi who had traveled so far. The Advent story is a hope story because it chronicles the coming to earth of the One who is hope, Jesus. For a people born in sin and for a world damaged by sin there simply could not be any other source of hope. Good education would not solve the problem. Benevolent government had no power to solve the problem. More and better laws couldn't penetrate to the source of the problem. People couldn't help one another, and they surely couldn't help themselves.

You see, the inescapable condition of sin infects every single human being and has scarred every aspect of the cosmos, which cried out for one thing and one thing alone: divine intervention. The only solution was a Savior, and the only suitable Savior with the wisdom, power, and righteousness to accomplish the task would be God himself. The One denied would come to rescue his deniers. The One rejected would move to save his rejecters. The One who had been rebelled against countless times would come to redeem the rebels. The One who had been replaced in people's hearts with an endless catalog of idols would invade the world he had made and rescue people from themselves. He would not come to set up an earthly kingdom and enforce his rule on the unwilling. He would not come to judge and condemn. He would not come demanding the service that was his rightful due. No, he came to serve, to suffer, and to die so that his kingdom would reign in the hearts of people. He came to seek and to save. He came to suffer and forgive. He came to rescue and restore. He came to call, draw, and love those who without his grace would continue to live for themselves. He came, and because he did, there is hope that sinners can be redeemed and the world can be renewed. It really is true: hope is a person, and his name is Jesus.

Before Jesus went to the cross to do what he came to do, he detailed for his followers why he is the only hope that could ever give hope to sinners. He made his identity and mission clear with these words: "I am the way, and the truth, and the life. No one comes to the Father except through me" (John 14:6).

In these brief words Jesus clearly explains why he is humanity's one and only hope.

1. Jesus is the way to God. Sin had created a horribly unnatural separation between God and the people he had created. God created people to dwell in loving and worshipful moment-by-moment fellowship with him. People were not designed to live independently. They were not made to figure life out on their own. People were meant to live according to God's will and for his glory. The great question of human history was, "How will this gulf between people and God ever be bridged?" Jesus came as the only possible answer to this question. He could meet God's moral requirement in every way by keeping his law without one instance of failure. He would be the final Lamb of sacrifice, paying the ultimate penalty for our sin. In his perfect life and acceptable death, he became the only way to restore relationship with God. He would return things to the way they were created to be.

2. Jesus is the truth from God. It is no exaggeration to say that Jesus came to earth as God's ultimate and final sermon. He didn't just communicate God's truth; he *was* God's truth. First, in a way that had never been done before, Jesus revealed the Father to us. He made the Father's character clear—so clear that he could rightly say, "Whoever has seen me has seen the Father" (John 14:9). But there's more: he revealed God's redemptive plan to us. Hanging on the cross, Jesus demonstrated how God planned to deal with our sin. He sent a Savior to die in our place. There's one final thing. The coming of Jesus preached the truth about our condition. We were in a state of impending doom, without any ability to rescue ourselves, so God sent Jesus as the ultimate, physical reminder of the depth of our need. Yes, it's true: Jesus is the truth from God.

3. Jesus is life. Jesus doesn't just preach life or provide life; he is life. Ephesians 2:1–2 talks about the dire condition we were in, apart from the person and work of Jesus: "and you were dead in the trespasses and sins in which you once walked." Dead people need life breathed into them or they will never rise and live again. Jesus came to be that life-giver. He came to conquer the ultimate result of sin: death. His resurrection was the firstfruit of a myriad of resurrections to come, as by grace his Spirit would breathe new life into all who would put their trust in him. He came as life to defeat the power of death and ignite eternal life in the hearts of his redeemed children.

Hope in the here and now and hope in the great forever that is to come rests on one set of shoulders. It rests on the almighty shoulders of Jesus, who is for you today the Way, the Truth, and the Life. He offers you what you have no power to provide for yourself: restored relationship with God, a knowledge of what really is true, and life that will never end. How's that for hope?

For further study: John 14:1–14

For parents and children:
Central theme: Jesus Is the Way

Ask your children what they think it means to say something like, "This is the way home" or "This is the way to school." Help them to understand that to say that Jesus is "the Way" means that he is the only road to God. Explain that the Christmas story is important because through the life and death of that baby in the manger we would have access to God, forgiveness from God, and acceptance into God's family.

December 11

The baby in the manger came as a conquering King to dethrone us and then to enthrone himself in our hearts and lives forever and ever.

If you have children or are around children, you know that you are in relationship with little self-anointed self-sovereigns, who think that the only authority they need in their lives is their own. Your little boy thinks of himself as king, and your little girl carries around with her the identity of queen. Children aren't born with a natural affinity for and commitment to the kingdom of God, because they are sinners. Sinners tend to see submission to an authority other than their own as a loss of freedom, and they tend to tell themselves that they have everything they need to successfully control their lives on their own. Sinners have a greater commitment to the kingdom of self than they do to the kingdom of God. They want to make their own rules and write their own stories. And they tend to constrict their daily field of concern to the small confines of their own desires, goals, choices, feelings, happiness, and needs.

Back to our children. We've all dealt with battles with our young children over what to eat, what to wear, and when to go to bed. That battle over what to eat doesn't happen because your three-year-old son read a book about the Paleo diet and decided that this is the way he wants to eat. In fact, your son knows nothing about a healthy and nutritious diet; that battle is not about food, it's about kingdoms. He is fighting not your cuisine but your authority. He is fighting to be king, that is, the only authority he has to follow. That battle your four-year-old daughter is willing to have with you over when to go to bed is not the result of a in-depth sleep study; it too is a battle for kingship (or should I say queenship?).

Let's get even closer to home. Why do you get angry in traffic or irritated when someone disagrees with you or envious when someone gets something that you would love to have? Because it's not just your children that battle for kingdom authority—you do too. You want to drive on unpopulated roads because few things are more important to you than your own schedule. You want people to agree with you because you want a kingdom filled with people who always recognize the brilliance of your thinking. Why do we all struggle with envy? We struggle with it because our greatest allegiance is to ourselves and our happiness.

There simply is no denying it: life this side of eternity is one big and unending war of kingdoms. Much of our inner turmoil and our interpersonal struggles are the direct result of kingdoms in conflict. Sin causes us to live inwardly directed, selfish lives instead of the lives of upward worship and outward love that we were created to live. Think about Adam and Eve. They were living in a glorious garden kingdom, where every need was supplied and God would come down and commune with them. They had it all, except one thing: self-rule. So they chose to step over the King's boundaries, taking authority into their own hands, while deluding themselves into thinking that it would be okay. Sadly, the results of that choice still live with us today. Reflect for a moment on how much of your anger in the last several weeks came out of your love for an allegiance to the kingdom of God. You and I don't tend to get angry with those around us because they have broken God's law. Rather, we are most regularly angry because the people broke our law, that is, the law of whatever makes us happy at the moment. In those angry moments, our problem is not that we are around difficult and disagreeable people; we have a kingdom problem, and blaming them misses the whole reason for the conflict.

So if Jesus came to be Savior, he also had to come to be King. I don't mean a monarch over a specific geographic area. Jesus had to rescue us from our bondage to our little kingdoms of one and usher us into his kingdom of loving authority and forgiving grace. He came to destroy our self-oriented kingdoms and dethrone us as kings over our own lives. In violent grace he works to destroy every last shred of our allegiance to self-rule, and in rescuing grace he lovingly sets up his righteous rule in our hearts. In grace he patiently works with us until we finally understand that truly good rule in our lives is his rule.

The baby in the manger came to be King, and he would not settle for anything else. That infant was the King of kings and Lord of lords. He would grow to be a man, a perfect man, who would talk again and again about the kingdom he came to establish; but he would do much, much more than just talk. The King would die as a criminal, so that criminals against his rule would be welcome into his throne room and live with all the rights and privileges of being members of his royal family. One of the glorious ironies of the biblical story is that the King—the king that we willingly love, worship, and serve—had to first die. Ordinarily the death of a conquering king is the end of the story. But this King came to conquer by dying for those over whom he would establish his rule. This is grace: the King died to dethrone kings so that he would be their King forever and ever and ever.

The baby wasn't wearing a crown and had none of the trappings of royalty, but don't be misled. He came to be King, and his kingship is your salvation.

For further study: Matthew 6:19–33

For parents and children:
Central theme: Kingdom
Get your children to talk about what they think a kingdom is. Help them to understand that sin causes us to set ourselves up as kings in our own little kingdoms. Talk to them about how Jesus was born not to make our little kingdoms work, but to invite us to a much, much better kingdom.

December 12

The baby in the manger came to tell us the worst news ever, because until we accept the worst news ever, we'll never want the best news ever.

The birth of Jesus was bad news. It wasn't just your typical piece of bad news; it was the worst news ever. Maybe you're thinking right now, "Paul, what in the world are you talking about? How could there be any better news than the coming of the Messiah to earth?" Well, you need to understand that there are two parts of the Christmas story, and you need both parts to make proper sense out of the whole story. The part of the story that tends to get the big billing (and it should) is the amazing, miraculous narrative of God putting on human flesh and coming to earth in the form of a baby. How amazing it is to think that God lay in that manger. God was suckled by Mary. God grew up in Mary and Joseph's house. God walked the dusty streets of Palestine. God endured hunger, rejection, physical pain, injustice, and yes, even death. Remember, the miracle of Jesus's birth is that he was fully God and fully man. God gave himself to us in outrageous redemptive love. God exposed himself to what we all face in this terribly broken and dysfunctional world. This story is so amazing, so beyond our normal categories for making sense of things, and so beautiful that it is hard to wrap the thoughts of your brain and the emotions of your heart around it. God has come to earth. Could there ever be better news than this?

But there is a second part of the story that makes God's shocking work of intervention make sense. Why would God do such a thing? What would motivate him to go to such an unthinkable extent? Whenever you see people do the unexpected or the unusual, it is natural to ask yourself why they thought that their radical action was necessary. This is where the Christmas story is the worst news ever. I'm going to ask you to humbly open your heart to this second part, the bad news part of the Christmas story. God has to invade our world in the person of Jesus because there was simply no other way. And why was there no other way? Prepare for the bad news. There was no other way because our big problem in life is not familial or historical or societal or political or relational or ecclesiastical or financial. The biggest, darkest thing that all of us have to face, and that somehow, someway influences everything we think, say, and do, isn't outside us; it's inside. If you had none of the above problems in your life, you would still be in grave danger, because of the danger you are to yourself. If the only thing human beings needed were a little external tweaking of their life circumstances, then the coming of Jesus to earth wouldn't make any sense. But if the greatest danger to all of us lives inside us and not outside us, then the radical intervention of the incarnation of Jesus is our only hope.

Sure, you can run from a bad relationship, you can quit a bad job, you can move from a dangerous neighborhood, and you can leave a dysfunctional church, but you have no ability whatsoever to escape yourself. You and I simply have no ability to rescue ourselves from the greatest danger in our lives. This means that without the birth of Jesus, we are doomed to be destroyed by the danger that lurks inside us from the moment of our first breath.

You don't need to look far in the Bible to know what this danger is. Its stain is on every page of Scripture. Romans 3:23 exposes this danger with a few simple words: "all have sinned and fall short of the glory of God." Sin is the bad news of the Christmas story. Jesus didn't come to earth to do a preaching tour or to hang out with us for a while; he came on a radical mission of moral rescue. He came to rescue us because he knew that we couldn't rescue ourselves. He knew that sin separates us from God and leaves us guilty before him. He knew that sin makes us active enemies against God, and what he says is good, right, and true. He knew that sin blinds us to the gravity of our condition and our dire need for help. He knew that sin causes us to replace worship of God with an unending catalog of created things that capture the deepest allegiances of our hearts. He knew that sin renders all of us unable to live as we were designed to live. And he knew that sin was the final terminal disease that, without help, would kill us all.

But the Christmas story tells us something more. It tells us that Jesus knew that even if we were aware of the great danger within us, in our own wisdom and strength we could not help ourselves. To every human being, sin is the ultimate undefeatable enemy. It captures and controls us all, and there is nothing we can do. It is either the height of arrogance or the depth of delusion to think that you are okay. None of us is okay apart from the invasion of grace that is the core purpose for the coming of Jesus.

Now, if you're like me, you have trouble believing this bad news. When you do something wrong, you probably try to blame it on stress or sickness, a bad boss, a troublesome spouse, a nerve-racking child, or just the generic pressures of life. When others come to you to point out a wrong, your initial response is probably not to be thankful. If you're like me, you jump to your own defense, because it's hard to believe that you're the sinner that they're describing.

So I want to encourage you today in a fresh way to accept the bad news of the Christmas story because, if you do, the good news becomes all the more comforting and glorious. The Christmas story tells you that you have been freed forever from denying or minimizing the danger that lives inside you because Jesus came to rescue you, forgive you, transform you, and ultimately to deliver you. That baby in the manger carried with him to earth everything that sinners need. It's only when you admit the need that you will be able to fully celebrate the solution that is Jesus.

For further study: Romans 5:6–11

For parents and children:
Central theme: Good and Bad News
Ask your children what they think would be the best news and then the worst news they could ever hear. Talk about how the Christmas story tells us the worst news ever (our sin) and the best news ever (the Savior came to purchase our forgiveness).

December 13

History marched toward his birth; that baby's life would march to his death, all so grace would march, with life and hope, into our lives.

I don't know whether you ever thought about this, but your Bible isn't arranged by topic. You might find that frustrating at times. You wish that the Bible were arranged by topic so that you could go directly to your subject of interest—if your Bible had topic tabs on the side of the page, that would be cool too. It's important to understand that your Bible is arranged the way it is not because of divine editorial error, but because of divine intention.

The Bible was never intended to be a systematic theology text, a compendium of helpful hints for everyday living or comforting maxims to carry you through your day. Your Bible isn't a collection of biographies that God uses as moral case studies. It isn't even proper to say that the Bible is a collection of historical stories of redemption. The core content of your Bible is one single story, a grand redemptive story. Maybe it's more accurate to say it this way: the Bible is one grand, theologically annotated story. The core content of the Bible is God's march of redemption accompanied by God's essential explanatory notes.

The story of the Bible wasn't written as a reaction but as God's intention before the foundations of the world were set in place. God knew Adam and Eve would step outside his wise and loving boundaries, and he knew what his response would be. You can see the seeds of that response in Genesis 3. What the Old Testament gives us is the history of God marching his world to the moment when the conditions were just right for the coming of Jesus. God calls Abraham and makes an eternal covenant with him. Out of Abraham God grows a nation, and out of the nation God sends the promised Messiah, Jesus. God promises to David a kingdom that will never end, and then Jesus as the final King. Even though his people are rebellious and disloyal, God will not forsake his grand redemptive plan. With sovereign authority and the unstoppable zeal of his grace, he harnesses the natural forces of the world he created and carefully controls the events of human history to march the world to the moment when Jesus would be born: Son of David, Son of Man, Son of God.

But Jesus's life was a march too. The destination of that march was written into the plot of God's redemptive story. Jesus knew where the march would take him, and he never debated, he never resisted, he never rebelled, and he never, ever questioned the plan. Every day of his thirty-three years of life he purposefully and willingly marched toward the cross of his death. He lived, loved, and taught with the pain of the horrible injustice in view. He marched with joy to his cross of shame, injustice, torture, and worst of all, separation from his Father because he knew what the results would be. He knew he was born to be the Lamb of sacrifice. He knew there were whips, nails, thorns, and swords in his future, all to be used as instruments of his suffering and death.

Who would knowingly and willingly take such a march? What innocent man would be willing to suffer in this way? Who in the world would be willing to do this for his enemies? Who would have such character? Who would be filled with such love? Who would be motivated by such grace? There is only one answer: Jesus. He is the One who occupies center stage in the grand redemptive drama. The march of redemption requires his march to his death, and he was willing.

Why was he willing? He was willing because he knew that his march to death was the only way to march life and hope into our lives. He knew that his painful, tortuous disgrace was the only way for redeeming grace to march with saving power into our lives. He knew the rescuing, restoring, and delivering power of that grace. He knew his march would result in a company of people, more than any human could number, who would give their lives to him and would in eternity bow in a chorus of worship of him forever.

So for the Bible to be something more than interesting stories and provocative sayings, it had to contain the real, historical march of history to the coming of Jesus, the march of Jesus to the cross and empty tomb, the march of grace into the hearts of countless sinners, and the march of those redeemed ones into an unending relationship of loving worship of the One who ordained the march before time began.

The Christmas story loses its meaning and beauty when it is ripped out of the great redemptive and historical march. It is more than a story of a family with nowhere to stay, singing angels, amazed shepherds, searching wise men, and a jealous monarch. If it were a made-up fable with all of these interesting elements, in the final analysis it would help no one. The Christmas story is not intended to teach you a bunch of moral lessons that require no history to be helpful. It's a story that is rooted in real history, real acts of God that are intended to provide for you and me the one thing we desperately need: moral rescue. The Christmas story is about a God of glorious grace on the march, invading human history with the grace of redemption. What was the cost of that grace? Well, the price was the death of his Son. What the birth of Jesus tells us is that, in love, both the Father and the Son were willing.

For further study: Galatians 4:4–7

For parents and children:

Central theme: Marching

Get your children to talk about what a march is and why people march. Help them to understand how God was marching the events of the world toward the coming of Jesus, and how from his birth in the manger the life of Jesus was marching toward his death on the cross to purchase our forgiveness.

December 14

When Jesus was born, the angels sang. When he died, graves opened. He lived to die. He died so we'd live.

I have a confession to make: I'm a very project-oriented person. I know exactly what I want to accomplish every day of my life, and I tend to do everything I do as fast as I can. Now, there is nothing evil about being project-oriented, but on any given day the tendency for me is to be more functionally committed to my plan and purpose than I am to the purposes of my Redeemer. In the midst of the drivenness of the day I become a God-amnesiac, and my thoughts, desires, and emotions are shaped by how well I am able to accomplish my sovereign plan for the day.

This way of living stands in stark contrast to the prayer Jesus taught us to pray and the heart he was calling us to have behind the words of the prayer.

Pray then like this:

"Our Father in heaven,
hallowed be your name.

> Your kingdom come,
> your will be done,
> on earth as it is in heaven." (Matt. 6:9–10)

This prayer is a call to surrender every moment, every location, every situation, every relationship, and all of my natural gifts and physical and spiritual capacities to the will of the King who has called me to his kingdom. What would happen if I would start every day by praying, "Your kingdom come, your will be done, this day as it is in heaven?" What would change in my marriage or parenting if I would pray, "Your kingdom come, your will be done, right here, right now in my marriage or with my children, as it is in heaven?" What would happen if I approached the ministry to which God has called me, praying again and again, "Your kingdom come, your will be done, right here, right now, just as it is in heaven"? Or how about surrendering my finances to God with this prayer: "Your kingdom come, your will be done, with all of my money and physical resources, as it is in heaven"?

The reality is that you and I are living either a life of demand or surrender. We are driven by our own agenda and the subtle (or not-so-subtle) demand that nothing or no one get in the way of what we want on any given day. Our demandingness is exposed by the quick anger we have in traffic that is delaying us, in the quick irritation we experience when someone disagrees with us, or the impatience we experience when someone causes us to have to wait. We quickly forget that God rules over every situation, location, and relationship for his glory and our good. And when we forget, we want control over things we will never control, and we tend to do and say things that we should not do or say.

You may be thinking, "Thanks, Paul, but what does this have to do with the thought that is at the beginning of this devotional?" Well, the song of the angels announced to the shepherds and to us the most amazing, most important surrender story ever. If anyone had a right to have his own way, in every way and all the time, it was Jesus. He wasn't just *acting* as if he were the Lord; he *was* the Lord. But in glorious and gracious surrender he didn't demand what was his right, but surrendered to the greater agenda of his Father. He was totally and unshakably committed to the plan, purpose, and will of the King. Everything he did, he did in surrender to the kingdom mission to which he had been called.

Jesus came committed to a death and resurrection mission. He came to give us life, but in order to give us life he had to be willing to die. He came with resurrection in view, but with the clear understanding that death always precedes resurrection. This death and resurrection mission was assigned to Jesus before the foundations of this world were laid in place. God's will was that Jesus would die to pay for our sins, but that the mission wouldn't end there. His death would be followed by the miracle of his resurrection, by which he conquered death and purchased life for all who would believe in him. The bursting open of graves at the hour of his death was a finger pointing to the resurrection power that was about to be released. The opening of those graves demonstrated that the cross and the tomb were not a defeat, but together are the place where sin and death are soundly defeated.

Here's what you need to understand. Without Jesus willingly living the prayer that he taught all of us to pray, the angels would have had nothing to sing about, those tombs would've never opened, sin and death would have never been conquered, and we would be the dead walking. Without Jesus living in the same surrender to which he now calls us, there would be no hope of the defeat of sin and no reality of eternal life for all who believe. It is true and valuable to remember that the gospel of Jesus Christ teaches us that the most wonderful things in life come to us not as the result of demand and control, but through sacrifice and surrender. Blessings that you could never achieve on your own come when you humbly and willing pray, "Your kingdom come, your will be done, right here, right now as it is in heaven." Aren't you glad that Jesus willingly did on earth what he taught us to do in this prayer?

For further study: 2 Corinthians 5:14–16

For parents and children:

Central theme: Demandingness

Get your children to talk about what it means to say someone is demanding. Ask them how and when they think they're demanding. Talk to them about how, if Jesus had demanded what was his right, he would never have been willing to come to earth and be born in that manger in Bethlehem.

December 15

The prophecy was our hope before we were born. A child would be born—Wonderful Counselor, Mighty God, Everlasting Father, Prince of Peace.

Perhaps no words more encouraging than these have ever been written:

For to us a child is born,
    to us a son is given;
and the government shall be upon his shoulder,
    and his name shall be called
Wonderful Counselor, Mighty God,
    Everlasting Father, Prince of Peace.
Of the increase of his government and of peace
    there will be no end,
on the throne of David and over his kingdom,
    to establish it and to uphold it
with justice and with righteousness
    from this time forth and forevermore.
The zeal of the LORD of hosts will do this. (Isa. 9:6–7)

There is no more stirring, encouraging prophecy of the birth of Jesus than this one. But I'm afraid that you can be familiar with this prophetic poem, because you hear it every Christmas season, and yet miss the core message of its words. Isaiah is saying more than that the Messiah who was to come would be wonderful in a variety of ways. Isaiah is preaching to us a truth that is way more profound, faith-stimulating, hope-giving, and life-altering than that. Take a moment right now to carefully examine and reflect on the names that Isaiah attaches to the Son to be born and the things he says about him. On reflection, did you see Isaiah's radically hopeful message?

With words carefully chosen, because they were carefully directed by the Holy Spirit, Isaiah is telling us that the Messiah Son is exactly what every sinner desperately needs. He is the ultimate answer to every destructive thing that sin does to us. Isaiah, with beautifully poetic words, declares to us that Jesus is all we need. He is the solution to the sin that we cannot avoid or escape. Long before we were born, God had appointed for us the One who would be the remedy for every symptom of the sin that would infect us all. Consider these words.

1. The government would rest on the shoulders of Jesus. What do sinners need? We need to be freed from the bondage of self-rule and welcomed to the rule of the One who is the definition of everything that is good, right, true, and loving. Jesus came to liberate us from the kingdom of darkness and transport us to his kingdom of love and light. This is essential, because our self-rule is our doom.

2. Jesus would be a Wonderful Counselor to us. Sin reduces all of us to fools. In our foolishness we see the world inside out and upside down. We look at what is false and see truth. We look at what is foolish and see wisdom. At the epicenter of our foolishness is a street-level denial of God—not philosophical atheism, but a denial of our need for God and a belief that we can live life on our own. As the Wonderful Counselor, Jesus comes to rescue fools from themselves.

3. Jesus would unleash almighty power on our behalf. Sin doesn't just reduce us to fools; it also renders us unable. So Jesus came to do by divine power what we could not do for ourselves. Sin causes us all to be unable to be what God designed us to be and to do what God created us to do. So Jesus would unleash his power to defeat sin and death and then empower us to desire and do what we would not be able to do without his power working in and through us.

4. Jesus would lavish on us his fathering care. Jesus, by his life, death, and resurrection welcomes us into his family once again. He is the door by which we have access to God. He lavishes his fatherly love, and we are blessed with all the rights and privileges of being his children. No longer separated, lost, alienated, and alone, we live forever as the sons and daughters of the King of kings and the Lord of lords.

5. Jesus's reign would be righteous in every way. In a sin-broken world, where all our lives are touched by the corruption, selfishness, and injustice of those who rule us, it is sweet comfort to know that the One who would establish his rule over us is righteous all the time and in every possible way. It is sweet to know that all corruption and injustice will end someday, and he will rule over us in perfect righteousness forever.

6. Jesus's rule would never, ever end. How sweet it is to know that the blessing of the grace of the King who was to come would never, ever end. His grace would never grow weary. His grace would never run out. He would rule in grace, giving us every needed grace, now and for all eternity. This means that hope now and hope then would no longer rest on our wisdom, our strength, our performance, or our track record, but on his unstoppable rule of grace.

7. God would make sure that what he promised would happen. And why can we bank on Isaiah's promises that all of our needs as sinners would be met in this way? We can bank on these things because God has placed his zeal upon every one of these promises. What does that mean? It means he will unleash his almighty power and authority to guarantee that all that was promised in the birth of Jesus would be delivered to each one of his children.

There is nowhere you and I can look to find better news than this. So much more than decorations, gifts, and lots of food, this season is about hope for sinners, carried into the world on the shoulders of Jesus.

For further study: Isaiah 7:14–15

For Parents and children:

Central theme: Prophecy

Define *prophecy* for your children (a prophecy is God's promise of what is to come). Talk to them about how many prophecies of Jesus's birth were made long before that first Christmas night. Help them to understand that the fact that all these promises about Jesus came true means that we can trust all the promises that God makes to us.

December 16

The suffering of Jesus didn't begin on the cross; it began in his straw bed and continued through to the cross, all for our redemption.

For he grew up before him like a young plant,
and like a root out of dry ground;
he had no form or majesty that we should look at him,
and no beauty that we should desire him.
He was despised and rejected by men;
a man of sorrows, and acquainted with grief;
and as one from whom men hide their faces
he was despised, and we esteemed him not.

Surely he has borne our griefs
and carried our sorrows;
yet we esteemed him stricken,
smitten by God, and afflicted.
But he was pierced for our transgressions;
he was crushed for our iniquities;

> upon him was the chastisement that brought us
> peace,
> and with his wounds we are healed. (Isa. 53:2–5)

In truth, that beautifully decorated tree, those gorgeously wrapped presents, and all that tasty holiday food, which make us happy during the Christmas season, are poor representations of the world into which Jesus was born and what his everyday life would be like. Jesus didn't show up for a celebration. He wasn't here for a vacation. His world wasn't well decorated, and he surely wasn't well fed. He came to a world that had been dramatically broken by sin, and his calling was to expose himself to the full range of its brokenness. This is where the details of Christ's birth are important. It means something profoundly important that the cradle of his birth was a feeding trough in a borrowed barn. You are meant to pay attention to the fact that he wasn't in a palace, attended to by servants. It's important to notice that the first smells that entered his infant nostrils weren't oils and perfumes, but animal smells.

These seemingly unimportant details set up a sharp contrast between our celebrations at Christmas and the true conditions of the Messiah's entry into our world. Most of us would be in a complete panic if we had to birth a baby in such conditions. But none of this was an accident. These conditions were God's plan. They announce to us that the Messiah came not to be served but to serve (Matt. 20:28). Since he came to rescue sufferers, it was essential that he suffer too. And his suffering wasn't reserved for the cross; it started the moment he was born. Everything he suffered was on our behalf. He would suffer but not lose his way. He would suffer and not quit and walk away. He would suffer and not grow bitter and angry. He would suffer and not respond with vengeance. He would suffer without thinking, desiring, saying, or doing even one wrong thing. He exposed himself to our world, to live as we could not live, so that as the righteous One, he could pay the penalty for our sin and give us not only peace with God, but a ticket to a future where suffering would be no more.

Don't let shiny ornaments and bright lights keep you from seeing the dark, sad drama of the life of that baby in that borrowed barn. Jesus experienced not one moment of ease in his life. Read the passage from Isaiah 53 again and let it sink in. Jesus wasn't good-looking in the way that would make him naturally attractive and popular. People regularly despised and rejected him. He was alienated from the very people he came to love and to rescue. His life was marked by sorrows and griefs of every kind. He willingly walked to his torture. He hung on that cross, body bruised, beaten, pierced, and broken. He did not look for escape. He did not selfishly use his power. He did not mock his mockers. He didn't do any of these things because he understood that suffering was what he came to do, and he was willing.

Jesus suffered because he did not demand what was his right; he endured what was wrong so that we may be right with God. The manger of his birth is a clue to what he came to do and what every day of his life would be like. The way God chose to rescue sufferers was by becoming a sufferer himself. Every moment of his suffering was done with us in view. Every dark moment of physical, relational, societal, and judicial suffering had a high and holy purpose to it: our salvation. You see, Jesus came to suffer because he came to be our Savior.

There's nothing wrong with the shiny ornaments and bright lights. Your celebration of what Jesus willingly did for you should be a festival of overflowing joy. So celebrate the blessings you've received, the best of those being the gift of Jesus, by passing that blessing on to others with gifts of love. Eat wonderful food, but let it remind you of the lavish spiritual food that God feeds you with every day because of the willing sacrifice of his Son, Jesus.

Here is what this means for you: commit yourself this Christmas to be a sad celebrant. Let your joy at what your Savior has gifted you with be mixed with grief at what it cost him. Remember this Christmas that you are celebrating the birth of the "Man of Sorrows." Remember as you celebrate that the One whom you celebrate enjoyed none of the things that likely make up your celebration (a house, beautiful things, fine food, etc.). This Christmas may your holiday joy be shaped and colored by remembering that you have eternal reason for joy because of the birth, life, death, and resurrection of your humble, willing, suffering Savior.

For further study: Luke 24:24–25, 46–49

For parents and children:
Central theme: Suffering
Ask you children to talk about what it means to suffer. Ask them why we all do everything we can to avoid suffering. Then tell them that the Christmas story is about Jesus being willing to come to earth to suffer, not because he deserved it, but because he loves us and was willing to suffer for our acceptance and forgiveness.

December 17

The coming of the infant King means the gracious destruction of the kingdom of self and a loving welcome to the kingdom of God.

It's the inescapable, destructive commitment of every person that was ever born. It marches down a pathway of separation from God and our ultimate doom. None of us successfully avoid it. We see it in others and it bothers us, but somehow we are blind to it in ourselves. It shapes what we think, desire, say, and do. It shapes our unwritten law for the people we live with and a host of unrealistic expectations for the situations we live in. It explains why we are so often irritated and impatient. It describes why some of us are perennially unhappy and some of us trudge through life depressed. It causes us to want what we will never, ever have and to demand what we do not deserve. It puts us at odds with one another and in endless fights with God. It is one of the deep diseases of our sin nature and a core reason for the birth of Jesus.

Paul says that Jesus came so "that those who live might no

longer live for themselves" (2 Cor. 5:14–15). Consider Paul's three-word description of what sin does to all people: "live for themselves." That's what we all do from the first moment of our lives. We all demand to be in the center of our world. We all tend to be too focused on what we want, on what we think we need, and on our feelings. We all want our own way, and we want people to stay out of our way. We all want to be sovereign over our lives and to write our own rules. We demand to be served, indulged, agreed with, accepted, and respected. In our self-centeredness, we convince ourselves that our wants are our needs, and when we do, we judge the love of God and others by their willingness to deliver them. When we are angry, it's seldom because the people around us have broken God's law; most often we are angry because people have broken the law of our happiness. Because we live for our happiness, happiness always eludes us—because every fulfilled desire is followed by yet another desire.

Now, I understand that this is not the stuff you want to be thinking about during the Christmas season. What I'm talking about isn't part of your typical holiday meditations. But what I'm talking about is an essential part of the drama, grace, and victory of the coming of the Messiah. As we celebrate the birth of Jesus, we also need to reflect on the violence of grace. What do I mean? Jesus came to decimate our self-oriented kingdoms of one so that he could welcome us to his glorious kingdom of wisdom, grace, and love. Grace destroys so that it can rescue. Grace destroys so that it can bless us with something much, much better. Grace destroys what has held us in bondage and frees us to live, love, and serve One greater than ourselves. Jesus came to endure a violent death so that in the violence of grace he could free us from the kingdom of self and transport us to his kingdom of life and light that will never, ever end. Now that's a story worth celebrating!

For further study: James 4:1–10

For parents and children:
Central theme: Selfishness
Get your children to talk about what it means to be selfish. Ask them if there is any place in their lives where they think they are selfish. Talk to them about how sin causes us all to live for ourselves. Tell them that the Christmas story is about God, in love, sending his Son to rescue selfish people from themselves.

December 18

The Son left his place in heaven so that God's sons and daughters would be guaranteed their inheritance in heaven. Amazing grace!

The Christmas story is a destination story. It's about an amazing journey that changed everything. It's a story about a place left and a place guaranteed. Only God could write this amazing story of the two destinations of grace. Consider how Paul summarized the Christmas story.

> Have this mind among yourselves, which is yours in Christ Jesus, who, though he was in the form of God, did not count equality with God a thing to be grasped, but emptied himself, by taking the form of a servant, being born in the likeness of men. And being found in human form, he humbled himself by becoming obedient to the point of death, even death on a cross. (Phil. 2:5–8)

The incredible destination story would not have happened, with all the resulting grace that flows to us every day, if it weren't for the sacrificial love of the Father and the humble willingness of Jesus. The loving generosity of the Father made him willing to send his Son from the glories of his perfectly holy place to the broken, dysfunctional environs of earth. And the Son didn't resist the call; he didn't fight for what was rightly his. He didn't negotiate the terms, and he didn't counter with a list of demands. I love how Paul captures it here: Jesus "did not count equality with God a thing to be grasped." You and I should be thinking right now, "Praise God, praise God, praise God that he didn't!" If Jesus had wrapped his fists around his rightful position of absolute equality with God, you and I, as sinners, would be without hope in life and in death. *If Jesus hadn't been willing to make earth his destination, we would have no hope whatsoever of the new heavens and the new earth being our final destination.* This is what we should be celebrating not just during the Christmas season but every single day of our lives. This willingness of the One who was God Almighty to leave the splendor of glory, to take on the normal limits and frailty of the human body, and to endure the daily realities of what it means to live in a terribly broken world is the definition of love.

It's important to ask what fueled the Messiah's earth-destination willingness. It's humbling to write this, but it's true: Jesus did what he did not because of something special he saw in us, but because of something holy and pure that was inside him. The Christmas narrative simply removes from every one of us any reason for boasting. There was not and is not one person who has any ability to earn or deserve the greatest gift that was ever given. In most gift-giving, there is something in the receiver of the gift that propels the giver. Maybe the person is your employee, and Christmas gives you an opportunity to say thanks. Perhaps the person has been a good friend for a long time, and Christmas is the time you recognize the investment he made in you over the years. Maybe it's just that the person is your relative, and the back and forth of gift-giving is a product of familial love.

But there simply was nothing in us to propel such a radical choice, such a radical gift that the Creator gave to the creatures who had turned their backs on him. Philippians 2 points us to the one and only thing that would ever make God willing to come to earth to rescue people who were more committed to worshiping themselves than worshiping him. In three words Paul tells us what motivated Jesus's journey from glory to earth: "he humbled himself."

You and I don't really expect powerful leaders to be humble. We expect a bit of arrogant swagger. We expect some boasting of accomplishments and an enjoyment of the results of acquiring power. But the Lord of glory didn't choose to bask in his glory; instead he emptied himself, took the form of not just a man, but of a lowly servant man. What humility! The Creator took on the body of a created man. The giver of the law submitted himself to the law. What humility! The King of kings placed himself under the rule of human kings. The One who owns everything was willing to live with virtually nothing. The One who is worthy of human worship willingly exposed himself to human rejection. What amazing humility!

Jesus's humility is our hope. His willingness to leave glory unleashed glory on us and guaranteed that we would live with him in glory forever. He made this broken world his destination so that our final destination would be a place where every form of brokenness has ended, and where we would live with him in a complete peace and harmony that will never end. But the humility of Jesus didn't end with his birth; it shaped the way he lived. He lived a humble, homeless life of daily service. The One whom creation was made to serve came not to be served, but to serve. It would have taken great humility for Jesus to leave his rightful place as God and live a lavishly rich life on earth, because no human wealth or power could compare with his rightful place. But he willingly emptied himself of all those rights and privileges, because he didn't come for himself—he came for us. But his humility didn't even end with his humble servant's life: Jesus's humility carried him to the cross. Without words or actions in his own defense, he humbly became the final sacrificial lamb, dying so that we would live.

So this Christmas remember that what you celebrate is a destination story. Jesus left what was his right, to guarantee for us a place that is not our right but is a gift from his humble hands.

For further study: 1 Peter 1:3–5

For parents and children:

Central theme: Destination

Help your children to understand what a destination is. Ask them to choose one destination that they would want to visit. Tell them that Jesus made earth his destination so that our final destination would be with him in the most wonderful place (new heaven and earth, where there will be no sin, sadness, or suffering) forever and ever.

December 19

The incarnation tells you who God is (perfectly holy, bountifully loving) and who you are (sinful, unable to escape). Believing both = hope.

Because we are made in God's image, we are hardwired for hope. You and I are always putting our hope in something. If you listen, you will realize that we communicate with the language of hope all the time.

"I sure hope it doesn't rain today."

"I hope she isn't mad at me."

"I hope I can do what I promised."

"I hope they win the championship."

"I hope they can get along for once."

"I hope this sickness isn't something serious."

"I hope when I get home, there will be something to eat."

"I hope I can do something worthwhile with my life."

"I hope what I've believed proves to be true."

I am persuaded that the language of hope is on our lips so much because we live in a world where hope seems temporary or is often dashed. In our work, in our families, as citizens, and in our own personal lives we all deal with so much broken hope. It's not unusual for the thing in which we willingly placed our hope to fail us. In fact, we get to the place where we're afraid to hope anymore, because we're sure we'll be disappointed once again. But we can't stop hoping, because God created our lives to be propelled and directed by hope, and he meant our capacity for hope to drive us to him.

Here's one of the things that I love about the Advent season and the Christmas story. If you look and listen carefully, this season will remind you where true hope is to be found. That freshly cut Christmas tree, with its beautiful pine aroma, should remind you that you can't put your hope in created things. Like everything in creation, the beauty of that tree will fade. It's inevitable that you'll find yourself dragging a dry tree to the curb, leaving a trail of dried-out pine needles behind you. People you celebrate with can't be your source of hope either because, if you know them well, you know they are weak and needy just like you. Even holiday joy can't deliver, because we all know that when the season is over, we all return to the realities of the world we live in.

Here's the best way to say it: the Christmas story reminds us that hope will never be found if you look horizontally. True hope is found only when you look for it vertically. It's not enough to say that God gives us hope. What the Christmas story declares to us is that God *is* hope. And that hope is attached to two glorious aspects of his character. First, God is *perfectly holy* in every way. It is the holiness of God that causes him to be angrily intolerant of sin. Now, I want you to think about God's anger. You could argue that God's anger is the hope of the universe. If God weren't angry about sin, there would have been no cross and no hope of salvation for sinners. You would not want to live in a world where the one ruling the world was incapable of righteous anger. God's anger with sin is a product of his holiness.

But there is more. God is not just perfectly holy, he is also *bountifully loving*. Because he is bountiful in love, God's anger with sin didn't cause him to wipe out sinful humanity forever, but to lovingly gift us with his Son to provide rescue, forgiveness, transformation, and ultimately deliverance. Jesus came to die, and it is on the cross of his death that the Father's holy anger and his bountiful love meet in a violent moment of righteous judgment and gracious redemption. God is your only source for steady, unshakeable, eternal hope. His holiness is your hope. His love is your hope. He is angry at what is destroying us, and in love he rescues us. The Christmas story preaches to us both the holiness and the love of God.

I have been arguing that true hope is only ever found vertically, but there is something I need to add. True hope won't be found without looking within yourself. You may be thinking, "How can I be to myself the hope that I need? Isn't that contradictory?" Well, if true hope is found in understanding who God is, the pathway to that hope is found in admitting who we are. You will never seek the vertical hope that only God can give if you don't first confess that you are a sinner. It's only when you humbly admit that you present empirical evidence every day that you have a wandering and rebellious heart that you will reach out for God's forgiveness and his transforming power. But you must admit to something else; you must admit that you have no ability on your own to escape. To say that you're a sinner is not just to confess to some wrong behaviors, but also to admit that you have a condition. Sin is a condition of your nature, and because it is, you can't escape it. You have no ability to run from yourself. The Christmas story confronts us with our inability, because if we had any ability whatsoever to save ourselves from sin, the birth of Jesus would not have been necessary.

The Christmas story reminds us that hopelessness is the only doorway to true and eternal hope. It's only when you give up on you that you seek and celebrate what God, in holy love, offers you in the person and work of his Son, the Lord Jesus Christ. It's true that hope isn't a thing; it's a person, and his name is Immanuel. Celebrate hope this Christmas.

For further study: Romans 5:1–5

For parents and children:
Central theme: Hope
Get your children to talk about what hope is. Ask them what their hopes are. Help them to understand that most of the things we put our hope in will fail us. Tell them that the Christmas story is a hope story. Help them to understand that Jesus came to give hopeless us hope that would never disappoint us.

December 20

Because sin has tragically infected all of us, the presence, work, and grace of that baby in the manger is what we all need.

You and I are very skilled and committed self-swindlers. Now I know that this is not how you would expect a Christmas devotional to begin. You would expect talk of angels, shepherds, a star in the sky, wise men, and a baby in the manger. But all of these story elements, which are so familiar to us, would not have been necessary without the single, dark reality we all work so hard to deny. From the moment of the very first sin in the garden of Eden, human beings have worked to deny what is true about them, that is, that we all desperately need what only God's grace can give us. We all swindle ourselves into believing that we are wiser, stronger, and more righteous than we actually are. We all walk around with an inner law firm that mounts a defense whenever we are accused of a wrong. And when we do this, we are denying our need for what the baby in the manger came to do for us.

If you're a parent, you see this truth played out among your children. Your son Danny has just hit his sister Suzy, so you go into the room and ask him why he would do such a thing. Danny doesn't say to you, "Mom, I do violent things because I have sin in my heart. You should expect even worse from me." In fact Danny doesn't talk about himself at all. When you ask Danny why he hit Suzy, he immediately begins to lay the blame for his violence against Suzy on Suzy! Danny has swindled himself into believing that the wrong he has done is not his fault and tells him nothing about who he is and what he needs. It really is possible to live in a state of Advent schizophrenia, where you celebrate the birth of the Messiah while actively denying your need for his birth, life, death, and resurrection.

So what we all need to confess is that denying our need for grace is more natural for us than confessing our need for grace. You know how it is: when someone confronts you, don't you find yourself immediately, silently in your mind, defending yourself? Have you ever had someone confront you, and your first thought was, "This is good, I need this, I wish they would do it more"? But there is something else we need to confess; if it is more natural for us to deny our need for grace than to confess it, then we need to humbly admit that it takes grace to confess our need for grace. If confession is owning personal responsibility for our words and our actions without excuse or shifting the blame, then it does take rescuing grace for us to come to the place where we admit our need for rescuing grace. Jesus came to provide that rescue.

Let me suggest four ways that we all tend to swindle ourselves into believing that we don't need the rescue that Jesus was born to provide.

1. We all tend to minimize our sin. We all have ways of naming our sin as something less than sin. We say we're not really mean—it's just our personality. We blame our poor attitudes on the weather, sickness, or busyness. We deny that our lies are lies. We tell ourselves that our lust isn't really lust, but enjoyment of the beauty of God's creation. With endlessly creative skill, we all tend to work to minimize the sin that we commit every day.

2. We all tend to doubt the wisdom of God's law. This is exactly what the Serpent worked to get Adam and Eve to do. We mount logical arguments for why it's okay for us to step over God's moral boundaries. Perhaps we say we're only going to do it this one time. Or maybe we tell ourselves that what we're doing really isn't what God meant by stealing. Perhaps we'll argue that it doesn't seem fair in a particular situation that we have to ________. The more we become comfortable with questioning the wisdom of God's law, the more likely it will be that we will feel okay with breaking those laws.

3. We all tend to be more concerned about the wrongs of others than our own sins. I know that on any given day I can be more engaged in, concerned with, and focused on the wrongs of the people I live and work with than I am my own. You will always deny your need for God's grace when you are more irritated than convicted. It's possible to be irritated with things in other people that you regularly excuse in yourself. It's possible to confront people with things that you minimize in your assessment of yourself.

4. We all tend to deny what's in our hearts. In some way, we all fail to accept the fact that sin is not just a behavior problem, but more fundamentally a matter of the heart. Sin is not just a matter of occasional wrong actions; it's a condition of our natures. It's not just that we sin; it's that we *are* sinners. When we tell ourselves that we can handle it, that we'll do better tomorrow, or that we don't need help, we're denying that sin is a matter of the heart, and because it is, we cannot escape it on our own.

So this Christmas, how about beginning your celebration with confession? I am convinced that when it comes to the redeeming work of Jesus, exuberant rejoicing begins with brokenhearted weeping. Only when sin breaks our hearts will the coming of the Messiah excite our hearts. And there's grace for this!

For further study: James 1:22–24

For parents and children:
Central theme: Self-Swindling
Define *swindling* for your children. (To *swindle* means to lie or

deceive to get something that you want.) Talk to your children about how we all lie to ourselves in order to think we're okay and what we do is okay. Help them to understand how we swindle ourselves by blaming the wrong things we do on other people or other things. Ask them where they tend to minimize or deny the wrongs they do. Help them to understand that when we deny our wrongs, we deny our need for what Jesus came to earth to do for us. Help them to understand that celebrating Christmas begins with confessing our need for the forgiveness that Jesus came to earth to give us.

December 21

The incarnation of Jesus Christ is a gracious rebuke to all who put their hope in human righteousness, wisdom, and strength.

Rebuke has a bad reputation. If I told you that I was going to come over in the morning and rebuke you, you probably wouldn't be very excited. When we think of rebuke, we envision pointed fingers, judgmental words, loud voices, and red faces. These things, however, have nothing to do with what rebuke is actually about. To be rebuked means to be compared to a standard and to be found lacking. Your morning mirror rebukes you because it confronts you with the difference between what you think you look like, or would like to look like, and what you actually look like. James 1:24 likens the Word of God to a mirror. Look into the mirror of the Bible and you will learn who you are, how you were designed to live, and what it is that you need.

The Christmas story confronts our delusions that we can live healthy and wholesome independent lives. If we were capable of being what we're supposed to be and doing what we're designed to do, and if we were able to solve our deepest and most foundational problems, then there would have been no need whatsoever for Jesus to take on human form, to be born as a baby, to live, die, and rise again. The Christmas story confronts us with our dependency. The Christmas story tells us that we need help. The Christmas story tells us that spiritual need and spiritual dependency are universal and inescapable. It makes no sense to celebrate the birth of Jesus when you strive for independence.

Here's what is important to understand: there are only two ways of living. You are either confessing that you were created by God to be dependent on his wisdom, power, and grace, or you are believing that you have within yourself everything you need to live well on your own. You are either doing everything you can to deepen your faith in yourself or you are preaching to yourself a gospel of personal need and divine provision. To build belief in yourself you have to convince yourself that you are more wise, strong, and righteous than you actually are and will ever be. We do this by comparing ourselves to the people around us, rather than to the perfect standard of God's law. The problem is that it is always possible to cite someone who seemingly is not as wise as you, not as strong as you, not as holy as you name yourself to be. Horizontal comparisons tend to stimulate self-righteousness. Think of the contrast between the words of the Pharisee and the tax collector in Jesus's parable in Luke 18.

> He also told this parable to some who trusted in themselves that they were righteous, and treated others with contempt: "Two men went up into the temple to pray, one a Pharisee and the other a tax collector. The Pharisee, standing by himself, prayed thus: 'God, I thank you that I am not like other men, extortioners, unjust, adulterers, or even like this tax collector. I fast twice a week; I give tithes of all that I get.' But the tax collector, standing far off, would not even lift up his eyes to heaven, but beat his breast, saying, 'God, be merciful to me, a sinner!' I tell you, this man went down to his house justified, rather than the other. For everyone who exalts himself will be humbled, but the one who humbles himself will be exalted." (Luke 18:9–14)

In comparing himself to other people who are obviously more sinful than he is, the Pharisee essentially tells God that he doesn't need him, and he surely doesn't need his forgiveness. How ironic it is to tell the One to whom you are praying that you don't need him. How strange is it to turn prayer into an argument for your independence rather than a humble confession of personal need. The argument of the Pharisee has two parts. First, he compares himself to others, and then he offers evidence that he is really quite righteous. Sadly, in this man's prayer, he is participating in his own deception—a deception that will be his doom.

The tax collector does just the opposite. Why is he so quick to cry out for God's mercy? He's quick to do so because he's looked into the mirror of God's Word. You cannot read God's Word without becoming deeply aware that you are a person in desperate need. You cannot read God's Word without being confronted with the sin that lives in your heart. You cannot read your Bible without facing the fact that you constantly fall beneath God's wise and holy standard. You cannot properly celebrate the Christmas story without also being willing to receive its clear and loving rebuke.

The birth of Jesus destroys the logic of human independence. It crushes the belief that our lives belong to us to live as we choose. The Advent narrative doesn't let you hold onto the belief that you can live as you were created to live without any power or wisdom but your own. The coming of Jesus levels the playing field. It puts us all in the same category. It doesn't matter if you're a man or a woman, young or old, where you were born, how much money or education you have, what race you are or what natural gifts you possess: if you are a human being, the Christmas story confronts you with the depth of your need for help. But the Christmas story doesn't just confront you with your need; it also introduces you to the ultimate helper. The Christmas story is about help coming to earth. He lay in that manger, and he will soon hang from a cross, all to provide for us the help we desperately need.

For further study: Philippians 3:1–11

For parents and children:

Central theme: Self-Righteousness

Help your children to understand the concept of self-righteousness—that we all tend to think that we're better than we are and that we all tend to excuse our wrongs. And when we do, we tell ourselves that we don't need help. Help your children to understand that the Christmas story confronts our belief that we are so good, we don't need help. God sent his Son because he knew that we are desperately needy and unable to help ourselves. Help your kids to understand that it makes no sense to celebrate the birth of Jesus while denying the reason for his birth and their need for what his life and death offers.

December 22

The incarnation of Jesus Christ is God's clear demonstration that he will always make good on all of his promises to us.

Read the huge comfort of Paul's argument in Romans 8:31–39:

> What then shall we say to these things? If God is for us, who can be against us? He who did not spare his own Son but gave him up for us all, how will he not also with him graciously give us all things? Who shall bring any charge against God's elect? It is God who justifies. Who is to condemn? Christ Jesus is the one who died—more than that, who was raised—who is at the right hand of God, who indeed is interceding for us. Who shall separate us from the love of Christ? Shall tribulation, or distress, or persecution, or famine, or nakedness, or danger, or sword? As it is written,
>
> "For your sake we are being killed all the day long;
> we are regarded as sheep to be slaughtered."

> No, in all these things we are more than conquerors through him who loved us. For I am sure that neither death nor life, nor angels nor rulers, nor things present nor things to come, nor powers, nor height nor depth, nor anything else in all creation, will be able to separate us from the love of God in Christ Jesus our Lord.

Paul powerfully argues that when God fulfilled his promise to send his Messiah Son to earth, he guaranteed that he would fulfill every other promise he's made to us. Paul also argues something else: the past grace of the birth of Jesus guarantees that we will receive the present grace that we daily need and the future grace that is our hope in this life and the one to come. How can you not love the comfort that comes from these words: "He who did not spare his own Son but gave him up for us all, how will he not also with him graciously give us all things"? What sense would it make for God to go to the extent of sending his Son to be born for our sake, and then to abandon us along the way? Since God was willing to make such a huge investment in his grace, isn't it logical to believe he will continue to invest in his grace until that grace has finished its work?

You see, the real historical events of the incarnation of Jesus are our guarantee that God will continue to deliver to us everything we need. We need divine rescue, we need forgiveness, we need to be transformed, and we need to be delivered. We need God's faithfulness, we need his patience, we need his wisdom, we need his power, we need his mercy, we need his rule, and we need his love. None of these things are at stake. None of these things will wear out. None of these things will quit working. God will never get tired of blessing us with these things. God will never get impatient and decide to quit. He will never get so irritated with the things we say and do that he'll turn his back on us and walk away. He will not get distracted or become weary.

Think about the fact that over the thousands and thousands of years between the sin of Adam and Eve and the birth of Jesus, God stayed faithful in every way and in every moment to his purpose to send his Redeemer Son. God exercised his power and authority to guide human, natural, and international events so that the time and circumstances would be as they needed to be for the coming of the Messiah. The biblical narrative is filled with hope. The years between the fall of Adam and Eve and the coming of Jesus present a powerful promise to us that God can be trusted. They tell us that no matter what it takes and how long it takes, God will always do exactly what he's promised to do.

But Paul preaches something more to us. He ends with this wonderful thought: if God was willing to send his Son to restore our relationship of love with him, you can be sure that he will not let anything separate us from his love. You see, the Christmas story is the world's best love story. It's about a God of love sending the Son of his love to live a life of love and die a death of love, so that all who believe in him would be welcomed into the arms of his love forever and ever. Embedded in the Christmas story is a promise of unbroken love for the children of God. You can do the dumbest thing, and God will still love you. You can have a day when you ignore his existence, and God will still love you. You can fail to do what he's called you to do, and he will still love you. I am not arguing that sin is okay or that you should not take it seriously. I'm arguing that the security of our relationship with God has never depended on the faithfulness of our obedience. If God withdrew his love every time we failed, there would be no hope for any of us. The unbreakable faithfulness of God's love for us is such a huge comfort precisely because we are unfaithful. The unstained perfection of God's love gives such hope to us because we aren't perfect.

The Christmas story is one big, beautiful promise. The fulfilled promise of Jesus's birth guarantees that God will, in his perfect timing and in his wise way, fulfill every other promise he has ever made to us. Past grace is your guarantee of present grace and of all the future graces you will ever need. And at the very center of the guarantee is the promise of God's eternal love. God sent his Son to us because he loves us. His Son now lives within us because God loves us. And we will live with him forever because God loves us. As you celebrate the birth of Jesus, celebrate the unbreakable love that his birth guarantees you.

For further study: Romans 8:18–39

For parents and children:

Central theme: Guarantee

Ask your children if they know what a guarantee is (an unbreakable pledge to do something for someone). Help them to understand that the Christmas story is God's guarantee that he will also give us everything that we need (not everything we want). If he gave us the amazing gift of his Son, Jesus, we can be sure he will give us all the other things we need to be what he wants us to be and do what he's called us to do.

December 23

What better reason to sing than this: the Savior is born to live, die, and rise again to fix what sin had broken.

The angels sang when Jesus came, but they're not the only ones who sing; we human beings sing. We can't stop singing. Children sing, and old men sing. People from every period of history sang. People from every place, of every race, and of every ethnicity sing. If you listen carefully, you will notice that we tend to sing about what has captured our hearts. We sing about what makes us sad. We sing about what makes us happy. We sing about people we love. We sing about our hopes and dreams. We sing about what's important to us. We sing silly songs about what makes us laugh. We sing about what makes us angry. We sing songs of love, exhortation, comfort, and warning. There's probably not a day in your life where you haven't sung or haven't heard a song. We sing; the question is, what song has your heart?

Could there be any more important song than the song the angels sang of the birth of the One who came as the hope of humanity? The song of the angels should make your heart sing. And may the songs of Jesus written since then capture your heart not only during this Christmas season, but every day of your life. Let the words of these songs about the birth of Jesus sink into your heart in a new way today. And may they help your heart to find rest and satisfaction in the person, work, and presence of Jesus!

"Hark the Herald Angels Sing"

Christ, by highest heav'n adored:
Christ, the everlasting Lord;
Late in time behold him come,
Offspring of the virgin's womb.
Veil'd in flesh, the Godhead see;
Hail, th'incarnate Deity:
Pleased, as man, with men to dwell,
Jesus, our Emmanuel!
Hark! the herald angels sing,
"Glory to the newborn King!"

Hail! the heav'n born Prince of peace!
Hail! the Son of Righteousness!
Light and life to all he brings,
Risen with healing in his wings
Mild he lays his glory by,
Born that man no more may die:
Born to raise the sons of earth,

Born to give them second birth.
Hark! the herald angels sing,
"Glory to the newborn King!"

"Joy to the World"

Joy to the world! the Savior reigns
Let men their songs employ
While fields and floods, rocks, hills and plains
Repeat the sounding joy
Repeat the sounding joy
Repeat the sounding joy

He rules the world with truth and grace
And makes the nations prove
The glories of his righteousness
And wonders of his love
And wonders of his love
And wonder wonders of his love

"O Come All Ye Faithful"

Yea, Lord, we greet Thee,
Born this happy morning;
Jesus, to Thee be all glory giv'n;
Word of the Father,
Now in the flesh appearing,

O come, let us adore him,
O come, let us adore him,

O come, let us adore him,
Christ the Lord.

"Silent Night"

Silent night, holy night!
Shepherds quake at the sight.
Glories stream from heaven afar
Heavenly hosts sing Alleluia,
Christ the Savior is born!
Christ the Savior is born

Silent night, holy night!
Son of God love's pure light.
Radiant beams from thy holy face
With the dawn of redeeming grace,
Jesus Lord, at thy birth
Jesus Lord, at thy birth

"O Come, O Come Emmanuel"

O come, O Rod of Jesse's stem,
From ev'ry foe deliver them
That trust your mighty pow'r to save;
Bring them in vict'ry through the grave.
Rejoice! Rejoice! Emmanuel
Shall come to you, O Israel!

O come, O Key of David, come,
And open wide our heav'nly home;

Make safe the way that leads on high,
And close the path to misery.
Rejoice! Rejoice! Emmanuel
Shall come to you, O Israel!

O come, our Dayspring from on high,
And cheer us by your drawing nigh,
Disperse the gloomy clouds of night,
And death's dark shadows put to flight.
Rejoice! Rejoice! Emmanuel
Shall come to you, O Israel!

"Thou Didst Leave Thy Throne"

Thou didst leave thy throne and thy kingly crown,
when thou camest to earth for me;
but in Bethlehem's home was there found no room
for thy holy nativity.

Refrain:
O come to my heart, Lord Jesus,
there is room in my heart for thee.

Thou camest, O Lord, with the living word
that should set thy children free;
but with mocking scorn and with crown of thorn,
they bore thee to Calvary.

When the heavens shall ring, and the angels sing,
at thy coming to victory,

let thy voice call me home, saying "Yet there is room,
there is room at my side for thee."

For further study: Psalm 95

For parents and children:
Central theme: The Songs We Sing
Tell your children that God commands us to sing (Eph. 5:18–19; Col. 3:16). Then ask them why God would think it's so important for us to sing that he would command us to do it. Help them to understand that singing focuses our hearts on what makes us happy, what makes us sad, what makes us laugh, and what we think is important. Ask them what their favorite Christmas song is, and sing a couple of their choices. Then help them to understand that there is nothing more wonderful to sing about than the birth of the One who came to earth to give us new life.

December 24

God entered the world, took on flesh, and defeated the Devil so we would no longer be defeated by the world, the flesh, or the Devil.

When you look into that manger in Bethlehem, you need to see a warrior. Jesus came to do battle with the Enemy and to defeat him for our sake. He would defeat the Devil in his life, he would defeat him on the cross, and he would defeat him by the empty tomb. Each victory was for us so that we would be able to resist the Devil's deceptions and temptations in our lives. Because Jesus came to defeat the Devil, a face-to-face battle with the Devil was inevitable. The life of the baby in the manger would march toward a moment when the Devil would throw everything in his arsenal toward Jesus. All of history hinged on that battle.

Soon that baby would grow into a man, and he would face what Adam faced: the seductive temptations of a deceptive enemy. He would stand toe-to-toe with Satan as the second Adam. The defeat of Jesus would spell our doom, but the victory of Jesus would guarantee our hope of countless moral victories as we too would face the seductive voice of the Tempter, whispering lies into our ears. You see, Jesus is the Chief Warrior, the Adam the world longed for, but the final battle is not over. We still live in a broken world that doesn't function as God intended. We still battle with temptation outside us and sin inside us. Seductive voices greet us every day, working to get us to step over God's moral boundaries. You could argue that life on this side of eternity is war. So it is a huge comfort that at Christmas we celebrate the birth of the second Adam, the Chief Warrior, who came to do battle on our behalf, to win victory for us, so that by his power we could resist, stand fast, and conquer. By grace Jesus was willing to come to earth and to stand in Adam's place, so that we would be graced with daily victory over temptation and sin. The Christmas story is the first chapter in a war story; this war was fought on our turf and for our sake by the hero of the story, the God–man, Jesus.

I want to contrast two historical moments for you. The first is that horrible moment when Adam and Eve faced the Serpent, bought into his deception, and rebelled against the wisdom, goodness, and authority of God. How could you possibly overstate the horrors of evil that were unleashed in that moment? The effects of that one act of disobedience are moral, emotional, rational, environmental, relational, political, and spiritual. Nothing in the created world was left unharmed. We still pay a daily price in the struggles of life and faith in this fallen world.

> Now the serpent was more crafty than any other beast of the field that the Lord God had made.
>
> He said to the woman, "Did God actually say, 'You shall not eat of any tree in the garden'?" And the woman said to the serpent, "We may eat of the fruit of the trees in the garden, but God said, 'You shall not eat of the fruit of the tree that is in the midst of the garden, neither shall you touch it, lest you die.'" But the serpent said to the woman, "You will not surely die. For God knows that when you eat of it your eyes will be opened, and you will be like God, knowing good and evil." So when the woman saw that the tree was good for food, and that it was a delight to the eyes, and that the tree was to be desired to make one wise, she took of its fruit and ate, and she also gave some to her husband who was with her, and he ate. Then the eyes of both were opened, and they knew that they were naked. And they sewed fig leaves together and made themselves loincloths. (Gen. 3:1–7)

Contrast this with another historical moment: the Christmas story is God responding to the cry of the world, now damaged and darkened by sin, for a second Adam. This Adam would need to be a perfect man, with the moral power to stand against the Enemy and not succumb to his tempting voice in any way. No person on earth was qualified to be the second

Adam, so God sent his Son, Jesus, to stand in that place for our hope and salvation.

> Then Jesus was led up by the Spirit into the wilderness to be tempted by the devil. And after fasting forty days and forty nights, he was hungry. And the tempter came and said to him, "If you are the Son of God, command these stones to become loaves of bread." But he answered, "It is written,
>
> "'Man shall not live by bread alone,
> but by every word that comes from the mouth of God.'"
>
> Then the devil took him to the holy city and set him on the pinnacle of the temple and said to him, "If you are the Son of God, throw yourself down, for it is written,
>
> "'He will command his angels concerning you,'
>
> and
>
> "'On their hands they will bear you up,
> lest you strike your foot against a stone.'"
>
> Jesus said to him, "Again it is written, 'You shall not put the Lord your God to the test.'" Again, the devil took him to a very high mountain and showed him all the kingdoms of the world and their glory. And he said to him, "All these I will give you, if you will fall down and worship

> me." Then Jesus said to him, "Be gone, Satan! For it is written,
>
> "'You shall worship the Lord your God
> and him only shall you serve.'"
>
> Then the devil left him, and behold, angels came and were ministering to him. (Matt. 4:1–11)

So tomorrow, when you celebrate Christmas Day, remember to celebrate the birth of the Great Warrior. He won the victory that you and I could have never won. That victory is our hope in this life and in the one to come.

For further study: Ephesians 6:10–20

For parents and children:
Central theme: War
Ask your children what they think war is. Then tell them that the Christmas story is a war story. Help them to understand that Jesus came as a warrior king to do battle with the enemy, Satan, and to win a victory that we could never win on our own. Remind them that the first man, Adam, battled with Satan and lost, so God sent Jesus to battle with Satan and win. Help them to see that Jesus came to earth to do this for us so that when we battle with Satan, we can win too.

December 25

The Wonderful Counselor lay in that manger, bringing heart-changing, life-giving wisdom to all who would put their trust in him.

All human beings are on a life-long journey to find wisdom, and all human beings want to think that they are wise. That three-year-old who endlessly asks "Why?" is in the process of putting pieces of a worldview together that will be the means by which she interprets and makes sense out of everything in her life. She's forming some kind of wisdom system that includes ways of thinking about her identity, the meaning and purpose of life, what relationships are about, where happiness is to be found, who God is, what's right and wrong, and a host of perspectives on other things. You see, from birth we are all philosophers, we are all theologians, and we all function like archeologists, digging through the mound of our existence to make sense of it all.

You may be thinking, "Paul, what does this have to do with Christmas?" Well, the Christmas story is a wisdom story, the best wisdom story ever told. No one was more aware that sin reduces all of us to fools than our Creator. I know that it's easier to see foolishness in someone else than it is to recognize it in yourself. It's the nature of foolishness. A fool is a fool because he hears his foolishness and thinks it's wisdom. So it's true of you and me and everyone else who has ever lived that sin turns us into fools. We see the world upside down and inside out. We have the sad ability to hear foolishness and think it's wisdom, to mistake falsehood for truth, and to confuse right with wrong.

But there's something even more dangerous and destructive about being a functional fool. Psalm 14 alerts us to the fact that at the epicenter of our foolishness is a denial of God. I don't think that the psalmist is talking about philosophical atheism. What he's alerting us to is the foolishness of living as if God doesn't exist or as if you don't need his authority, wisdom, power, and grace. Every time you take your life into your own hands and do whatever you want to do no matter what, you are functionally denying the existence of God. Every time you make decisions as if your life belonged to you, you are denying the existence of God. Every time you buy into the delusion of independent wisdom, righteousness, and strength, you are telling yourself that you can live quite well without the presence, power, and grace of the One who made you. Every day that you live without God in your thoughts and his glory as your core motivation, you functionally deny the existence of God.

God not only knew that in our foolishness we would tend to be more attracted to what is not true than what is true, but he also knew that our foolishness would make us forget him rather than make him the hope of our hearts. So here is another way to think of the Christmas story: our God of wisdom sent his Son, who is wisdom, to shed his grace on fools so that by his grace they would be rescued from themselves and become wise. A fool has no ability whatsoever to rescue himself from his own foolishness. A fool is always a person in need of external rescue. The Christmas story is about God being willing to provide that rescue.

Listen to how Paul talks about God's gift of the One who is Wisdom.

> Where is the one who is wise? Where is the scribe? Where is the debater of this age? Has not God made foolish the wisdom of the world? For since, in the wisdom of God, the world did not know God through wisdom, it pleased God through the folly of what we preach to save those who believe. For Jews demand signs and Greeks seek wisdom, but we preach Christ crucified, a stumbling block to Jews and folly to Gentiles, but to those who are called, both Jews and Greeks, Christ the power of God and the wisdom of God. For the foolishness of God is wiser than men, and the weakness of God is stronger than men.
>
> For consider your calling, brothers: not many of you were wise according to worldly standards, not many

> were powerful, not many were of noble birth. But God chose what is foolish in the world to shame the wise; God chose what is weak in the world to shame the strong; God chose what is low and despised in the world, even things that are not, to bring to nothing things that are, so that no human being might boast in the presence of God. And because of him you are in Christ Jesus, who became to us wisdom from God, righteousness and sanctification and redemption, so that, as it is written, "Let the one who boasts, boast in the Lord." (1 Cor. 1:20–31)

So as you celebrate this year, remember that Wisdom is a person, and his name is Jesus. He was born to rescue fools like you and me. That's something worth celebrating!

For further study: Titus 3:1–11

For parents and children:
Central theme: Foolishness
Ask your children to tell you what they think a fool is or what it means to be foolish. In the Bible a fool is someone who thinks he's so wise that he does not need God's Word or God's help. Help your children to grasp that Jesus came to earth on that Christmas night to rescue fools. Let them know that one of the names of Jesus is Wisdom. Help them to see that sin turns all of us into fools who want our own way and resist God's help. Then tell them that at Christmas God sent Wisdom to earth to rescue us (fools) from ourselves.

December 26

The coming of the sovereign Savior means the end of self-rule and a welcome to submit to the plans and purposes of One greater.

It is so amazing, so beyond the scope of how we tend to think about why things happen in the way that they happen, and so different from the way that we access our lives, that it is hard for us to grasp its full scope and practical meaning. Generation after generation, theologians have worked to make sense of it. The Bible declares that God is in absolute, unchallenged control of everything in the universe that he created.

The Bible declares that God controls the forces of nature.

> He gathers the waters of the sea together as a heap;
> he puts the deeps in storehouses. (Ps. 33:7)

> Are there any among the false gods of the nations
> that can bring rain?
> Or can the heavens give showers?
> Are you not he, O Lord our God? (Jer. 14:22)

The Bible declares that God rules human governments.

> Let the nations be glad and sing for joy,
> for you judge the peoples with equity
> and guide the nations upon earth. (Ps. 67:4)

> The king's heart is a stream of water in the hand of
> the LORD;
> he turns it wherever he wills. (Prov. 21:1)

The Bible says that God controls the details of our individual lives.

> And he made from one man every nation of mankind to live on all the face of the earth, having determined allotted periods and the boundaries of their dwelling place. (Acts 17:26)

The Bible declares there is nothing that is not under God's control.

> For his dominion is an everlasting dominion,
> and his kingdom endures from generation to
> generation;
> all the inhabitants of the earth are accounted as
> nothing,
> and he does according to his will among the
> hosts of heaven
> and among the inhabitants of earth;

and none can stay his hand
or say to him, "What have you done?"
(Dan. 4:34–35)

Here is the amazing truth of the Christmas story: that baby in the manger is the sovereign Savior come to earth. The One who rules everything that ever was now humbly and willingly places himself under human rule. The One who controls everything exposes himself to the forces of nature and the governments of the people he established and rules. The King of kings and Lord of lords comes to live a life without political power or a palace in which to reign. Human rulers will mock, reject, persecute, and ultimately kill him. Nothing in the way he lived his life would make you think that he was the King of kings. He lived humbly and in poverty. He not only didn't establish earthly rule—he didn't even have a house that was his own.

The Christmas story confronts us with this question: "Why would the Lord of lords debase himself in this way?" Answering this question pushes us to the heart of what this story is about. Jesus didn't come with royal pomp, demanding to be served. His plan was not for political power or palace living, because he was on a single, focused mission, and no amount of poverty, homelessness, or rejection would deter him from his mission. What was this mission? What I'm about to say will probably hurt your feelings. The sovereign Savior came to earth because sin causes all of us to live as self-appointed self-sovereigns. We all put ourselves in the center of our world. We all are way too focused on what we want, what we feel, and what we think we need. We all want control over things that we will never control. We all get angry when someone or something gets in the way of our self-designed sovereign plans. We all want to write our own rules, and when we break God's rules, we want to be able to do it without negative consequences. We go through days without consciously thinking about God's will or his glory. We allow our hearts to be captured by the idol of idols: self. When you buy into your own sovereignty, you not only compromise your spirituality, but you also lose a piece of your humanity.

We were made to live under God's rule. To recognize and submit to God's sovereignty isn't a loss of freedom; it is the only pathway to true human freedom. To try to establish your own sovereignty is like trying to drive a boat down a highway: it's not what you were designed to do, and it will not result in the life that you were created to live. Jesus willingly humbled himself and lived in poverty, rather than sovereignty, so that through his life and death he would rescue self-sovereigns from themselves. He placed himself under broken and unjust human rule in order to liberate us from self-rule and transform us into people who celebrate and willingly submit to his rule.

God exercised his sovereignty over all things in order to set up the right time and right place for the sovereign Son to be born as a man, live perfectly, die acceptably, and rise victoriously. By sovereign power he assured that everything would happen according to the plan formed before the earth was created. By his sovereign will he ordained that this story of stories would be written down and preserved for us. And by sovereign grace he calls us to himself, opens our eyes to his glory and grace, convicts us of our sin, forgives us, welcomes us into his family, transforms us by his grace, and expends his power to keep us for all eternity. The sovereign Son became a submitting man so self-sovereign sinners would be rescued from themselves and become those who love and submit to his rule. Remember today that the Christmas story is a sovereignty story, and because it is, you and I have hope of real life and true freedom!

For further study: Philippians 2:1–11

For parents and children:
Central theme: Sovereignty
Define *sovereignty* for your children (it means that all things are under your rule and control). Get them to talk about places in their lives where they want sovereignty (don't want to be told what to do, don't want to share possessions, don't like it when someone is in their way). Help them to understand that there is only one sovereign ruler in the world, and it will never be us. Help them to see that the Christmas story is about a sovereign King, Jesus, coming to earth, not to rule, but to suffer for our sakes. Then help them to understand that Jesus was willing to do this so that he could set up his rule in our hearts, because we are not capable of ruling ourselves.

December 27

The coming of the child who would give his life means abundant life and eternal life for all who put their trust in him.

No, it wasn't a zombie apocalypse. The Creator and Giver of life came to the world he had created and found dead people walking around everywhere he looked. How sad it must have been for Jesus, who breathed life into humanity, to be face-to-face with dead humanity. And how sad it was for him to recognize that although they were dead, they didn't know they were dead, and because they didn't know, they didn't hunger for the life that he had come to give them. How sad it is to have the one thing people desperately need, but they're not interested in what you have to offer.

Life was born in that manger; it's what the Christmas story is about. Life was born among the dead so that the dead would come to life. Now, I'm not talking here about physical death, but rather spiritual death. But consider the power of this word picture. This may sound crass, but it confronts us with what it means to be spiritually dead: the one person you expect nothing from at a funeral is the deceased. Because the person is dead, he is unable to relate to you, let alone rescue himself from his sad state. Consider that:

1. A dead man has no awareness that he is dead.
2. A dead man has no ability to cry out for help.
3. A dead man can't breathe life into himself.
4. For a dead man to live, a divine miracle must take place.

Listen to the description in Ephesians 2:1–9 of every sinner apart from the life-infusing grace of the Messiah, Jesus:

> And you were dead in the trespasses and sins in which you once walked, following the course of this world, following the prince of the power of the air, the spirit that is now at work in the sons of disobedience—among whom we all once lived in the passions of our flesh, carrying out the desires of the body and the mind, and were by nature children of wrath, like the rest of mankind. But God, being rich in mercy, because of the great love with which he loved us, even when we were dead in our trespasses, made us alive together with Christ—by grace you have been saved—and raised us up with him and seated us with him in the heavenly places in Christ Jesus, so that in the coming ages he might show the immeasurable riches of his grace in kindness toward us in Christ Jesus. For by

> grace you have been saved through faith. And this is not your own doing; it is the gift of God, not a result of works, so that no one may boast.

Because we were dead in our sins, we were completely without any ability to rescue ourselves. We were stuck in our sins and trapped in a cycle of rebellion against God, slaves to our passions and objects of God's wrath. Not only were we dead, but we were also doomed, and not only were we doomed, but we were also helpless. Here you find the essence of the Christmas story. Here is where it preaches to us about God's abounding love and his amazing grace. Because we were not able to act for ourselves to change our condition, God acted on our behalf. And because he is boundless in love and plenteous in mercy, he acted *for* us and not *against*. If God had acted against us, his judgment would have been right—we deserved his wrath. But the birth of Jesus told the world of dead people that God was not going to act in anger but in mercy. He was not going to mete out punishment but rather grace. He wasn't going to strike us with his holy sword of vengeance but rather gift us with his life-giving Son.

The birth of that baby tells you that the story of humanity would not end with the walking dead. It would not end with slavery to sin and separation from God. The birth of Jesus is God acting radically in human history to give life to dead people. How would that happen? Well, the One who *was* life would take on all our sin and die so that we would not only have life right here, right now, but fullness of life with him for all of eternity. The One who is life died for the dead so that the dead would have life forever.

The birth of Jesus tells you something else. Because of what Jesus would do in his life, death, and resurrection, because he was willing to die to give life, we will live, but death will die. The birth of the ultimate life-giver, Jesus, guarantees the death of death. In the life and work of that baby in the manger all the effects of sin will be defeated, the worst of them being death. As the children of God, we will not only live, alive in heart and alive to God, but we will be invited to the one funeral we'll actually want to go to. We'll be invited to the funeral of sin and death, because sin and death will die because of the redeeming work of the One born in Bethlehem.

So this Christmas remember that beneath the angels, the shepherds, the wise men, Mary and Joseph, and that rented barn is this amazing story of life and death. And because it's a story of life and death, it's a story of amazing grace. The birth of Jesus is a sure sign that God will act where we cannot act, and he will act with life-giving grace. Celebrate that Jesus came to give life, because it's the one gift we could never, ever give ourselves.

For further study: Galatians 2:19–21

For parents and children:

Central theme: Alive

Ask your children how they know when something is dead and how they are sure that something is alive. Help your children to understand that apart from what Jesus came to earth to do, we are dead in our sins. That means that what we were created to be and to do, we have no power to be and to do. So Jesus was born in that manger in order to give life to dead people. Help them to see that Jesus makes us alive so that we can know him, trust him, and have the power to serve him.

December 28

The baby in the manger came because the world was (and still is) groaning, waiting for its final redemption.

I have a confession to make: I love food. Don't misunderstand me; I'm not saying that I love to eat huge amounts of food. What I love is the seemingly endless catalog of sights, sounds, and tastes of food. I love a meal that has a variety of textures and takes you on a wide-ranging taste ride. I love the applied chemistry of food. I love how heat, cold, oil, water, spices, yeast, and a whole bunch of other things change not only the taste, but the composition of whatever it is that you're cooking. I love cooking tools, from a good set of knives and pans to smoking guns and Sous-vide machines. I love going to a restaurant where I know the chef respects good ingredients and knows how to manipulate them, and I love cooking a fine dinner for people and enjoying their enjoyment.

Now you may be thinking, "What does this have to do with the statement at the beginning of this devotional?" Well, one of the reasons why we groan is that we are spiritually hungry.

All of the things that we have consumed, which we thought would satisfy us, haven't. We have been eating, but the food has left us empty. If you're physically starving, you will groan, but spiritual starvation will make you groan too. So here's the good news of the Christmas story: the birth of Jesus is an invitation to the best, most satisfying dinner ever.

The Bible is not alien to the world of food. In fact, feeding the hungry with good food is one of the primary ways that the Bible talks about the gospel of the redeeming grace of Jesus. The Bible lets me know that God recognizes my hunger and that he promises to do what is necessary to satisfy it. But the Bible is even more direct when it comes to our spiritual hunger. It tells us that Jesus is the only food that will ever satisfy the needy, groaning hunger that is in the heart of every one of us. The birth of Jesus is an invitation to finally have your spiritual belly filled with the most beautiful, hunger-satiating food ever. Consider these passages:

The promise of satisfying spiritual food. "The afflicted shall eat and be satisfied; those who seek him shall praise the Lord! May your hearts live forever!" (Ps. 22:26). "Afflicted" in this passage means poor. One of the harsh realities of poverty is hunger. Sin makes us spiritually poor, and God promises to satisfy that hunger.

The invitation to feast and be satisfied. "Come, everyone who thirsts, come to the waters; and he who has no money, come, buy and eat! Come, buy wine and milk without money and without price. Why do you spend money for that which is not bread, and your labor for what does not satisfy?" (Isa. 55:1–2). Here is both an invitation to eat spiritually satisfying food that someone else has paid for and an exhortation, in the form of a question, to quit eating what can never spiritually fill you.

The illustration of what food satisfies, and what doesn't truly satisfy. (Read John 6:1–14.) It was an incredible satisfying miracle meal. Jesus fed more than five thousand people with a boy's lunch, but the people missed the point Jesus was trying to make. Even though the crowd had been miraculously fed, they would soon be hungry again. The problem with a good physical meal is that it won't be long before you're hungry for another one. Then Jesus said, "Do not work for the food that perishes, but for the food that endures to eternal life, which the Son of Man will give you" (John 6:27). Jesus is saying, "I am the only one who can give you a dinner that will satisfy your hunger forever."

The only food that satisfies. "And he took bread, and when he had given thanks, he broke it and gave it to them, saying, 'This is my body, which is given for you. Do this in remembrance of me'" (Luke 22:19). "I am the bread of life; whoever comes to me shall not hunger, and whoever believes in me shall never thirst" (John 6:35). The birth of Jesus is not only an invitation to the best dinner ever, but it is also the delivery of the food that will be served to the very hungry person who comes to God's table. Jesus is that food.

The celebration dinner. "And the angel said to me, 'Write this: Blessed are those who are invited to the marriage supper of the Lamb.' And he said to me, 'These are the true words of God'" (Rev. 19:9). Our invitation to this celebratory dinner where we have been forever united to Christ is written in his shed blood. He is not only the food that satisfies, but also the sacrifice that pays the price for us to be part of the final dinner that will never, ever end.

Jesus was born because God cared about our hunger. Jesus was born because God knew that nothing in creation would ever silence our growling stomachs. Jesus was born to invite us to the ultimate meal that would finally satisfy the hunger of our hearts. And Jesus, in his life and death, paid the price that we could never afford to pay, so that we could sit at the banquet table of his grace and finally be satisfied. Yes, it really is true: the birth of Jesus is not only an invitation to dinner, but also the gift of the food that every spiritually hungry person is by grace invited to eat, so that with full hearts we would groan no more.

For further study: 1 Corinthians 11:23–26

For parents and children:
Central theme: Hunger
Ask your children what it means to be hungry and how they know that they are hungry. Ask them what their favorite food is or what their favorite Christmas food is. Then help them to

understand that we all experience two types of hunger: physical hunger and spiritual hunger. Help them to understand that not only do our bellies get hungry, but our hearts are hungry as well. Just as our bellies groan when they are empty, our hearts groan to be filled too. Then help them see that Jesus was born to be the only spiritual food that would ever satisfy the hunger of our hearts. Tell them that the Christmas story is about the coming of the Bread of Life so that our hearts would be hungry no more.

December 29

Jesus was born to die in our place so that we who were dead would be born again to new life.

Jesus was born to give us life. The Christmas story has all the drama of a death-to-life story, because the baby in the manger came to die in order to give life to all who believe in him. If you have placed your hope and trust in the Messiah, Jesus, you know he came to give you life. But here is the burning question: what do you think that means? I think many of us have a strong belief and understanding in salvation past, the forgiveness we have received in Christ, and many of us have a pretty sturdy hope of salvation future, the eternity we will spend with Christ, but we are not as sure about the present benefits of the work of Jesus in the here and now. I am afraid that many of us have a big gap in the middle of our understanding of the gospel.

One of the beautiful things about the Christmas story is that it doesn't offer just my past forgiveness and future hope, but everything I need right here, right now. Jesus came so that

I would have everything I need to fight the discouraging battle with private sin. Jesus came so that I would have everything I need to have a peaceful relationship with my angry neighbor. Jesus came so that I could stand against the temptations of racism and prejudice. Jesus came so that I could forge with my spouse a marriage of unity, understanding, and love. Jesus came so that I could parent my children with patient wisdom and grace. Jesus came so that I could face the realities of life in a fallen world without doubt or despair. Jesus came so that I would be granted not only the promise of daily forgiveness, but also the promise of fresh starts and new beginnings. Jesus came so that the hate in my heart would be replaced with love and the anger in my heart would be replaced with peace.

I love how Peter captures the now-ism of the work of Jesus Christ for each one of us. "His divine power has granted us all things that pertain to life and godliness" (2 Pet. 1:3). With the heart of a good pastor, Peter starts his letter to people who are facing hardship with a reminder that in Christ they have *already* been given *everything* they need to face *whatever* they are facing. He says that they have been given everything they need for *godliness*. Now what is this thing called godliness? Godliness is living a God-honoring life between the "already" of my conversion and the "not yet" of my final home-going. Peter knows how important and life-changing it is to know and believe that Jesus came so that we would have all that we need to live as he intended right now. Understanding and believing this will change you and the way you live. If you do not carry this identity with you, you will look to people and things to give you identity. If you do not have this hope, you will look for hope where lasting hope cannot be found. If you don't carry this assurance with you, you will live with unrest in your heart. If this reality isn't the foundation of the way you approach life, you will live on a constant search for wisdom and strength. The ultimate gift, Jesus, was given so that you and I would have all the things we need to face all the things we encounter between the moment we first believed and the moment of our last breath. Now that's a story worth celebrating!

But I want to say more. The right here, right now grace of Jesus frees us from those things that tend to capture our hearts and derail our living. He came so that we would be free from the power of:

1. *Fear.* Many of us are afraid of being known or afraid of honestly facing what's inside us. Here's the good news of the right here, right now benefits of the birth of Jesus. There's nothing that could ever be known, exposed, or revealed about you that isn't covered by the present grace that is yours because of the life, death, and resurrection of Jesus.
2. *Regret.* Many are rendered timid or even paralyzed by choices, failures, and sins of the past, and when you are, you carry around a heavy load of guilt and you tend to hide in shame. The right here, right now

forgiveness of Jesus not only liberates you from the past, but also welcomes you to fresh starts and new beginnings.

3. *Discouragement.* Many of us are simply overwhelmed by what's on our plate. We feel unable, and we think we are doomed to failure. God's right here, right now grace assures us that God will never call us to a responsibility without also gifting us with what we need to do what he has called us to do.
4. *Denial.* Many of us are tempted to grab for peace by denying the dark things that are still inside us and the struggles that are outside us. But the right here, right now grace of Jesus frees us from having to play monkey games with the truth. Jesus's works assure us that whatever we're facing, we're not alone and we have help that is way beyond our limited personal resources.
5. *Desire for control.* Many of us wake up each morning wishing we had more control so we could free ourselves from what we find difficult. The right here, right now grace of Jesus assures us that the One who was born on Christmas now rules over all things for our sake. Our lives may be out of our control, but they are always under his control.

So as you celebrate Christmas, celebrate the abundant life that is yours today because of the birth of that baby in the manger.

For further study: 2 Peter 1:3–9

For parents and children:
Central theme: Abundant Life
Help your children to understand that Jesus didn't come to earth to give us just eternal life, but abundant life right here, right now where we live every day. Ask them if they know what *abundant* means and then define it for them (it means filled to overflowing). Help them to see that Jesus was born so we would have life to the fullest—not just in the future, but right now. Help them to see that the birth of Jesus is God's promise to us that he will fill us with every good thing we need until we are finally home forever with him.

December 30

God became a child so that through his life, death, and resurrection, we might become the children of God.

I love a good novel. I love to watch a skilled author carefully and creatively develop the personality profile and the backstory of every character. I love how the author paints each scene and location with well-chosen words. I love the twist and turns, the surprises, and the building of the drama of a well-crafted plot. And I love how the novelist can take you away to another place and paint pictures in your mind that, as you read, seem more real than the real things around you. There is nothing like a good story.

I decided to write this Advent devotional because I'm persuaded that our lives are defined by story. There is always some big, overarching story that becomes your tool for understanding your personal story. For my dad, World War II was the defining story of his life, and he never let go of that story until the day he died. For my mom, the story of growing up in a very large and sadly abusive home was an influential, identity-shaping story in her life. Maybe for you it's the story of an ancestor's immigration to America or the story of economic loss. Maybe it's the story of an accident, illness, or injury that has had power to define you. Or it could be the story of life in the inner city or in the suburbs that interprets for you who you are. We all carry stories with us, and the stories that we carry become the means by which we make sense of the individual stories that we live every day.

So I decided to write this devotional so you would carry with you the greatest true story ever told. I wrote this devotional so you would embed your little personal story in the larger story of redemption. My hope in writing is that this devotional would stimulate you to live with a birth-of-Jesus mentality. My prayer is that the story of the birth, life, and sacrifice of Jesus would be *the* story that would shape everything in your life. I hope that whether it's your finances, your marriage, your work, your sexual life, your friendships, your education, your leisure, or your future, that you would make sense of every dimension of your life through the lens of what the Christmas story tells you about life.

Because the Christmas story is meant to help you interpret and understand your story, it's important to slow down and take time to meditate upon this amazing story of mind-blowing grace. I love the work of the abstract expressionist painters, and one of my favorites is Barnett Newman. So I was excited when I learned that the Museum of Modern Art in New York City was showing an extensive exhibit of Newman's work. The masterpiece of the exhibit was a painting entitled *Vir Heroicus Sublimis* (Man, heroic and sublime). *VHS* is 7'11" tall and 17'9" wide. It is a stunning field of red, but not just a single layer of red; layer after layer of thinned red paint makes you feel that you could step into the red world that is before you. Newman instructed the viewer not to stand way back from the painting to view it, which is your instinct when you try to view a huge canvas. Newman wanted you to get as close as the museum would allow, so that you would feel that you were being enveloped by a sea of gloriously bright and endlessly deep red. So when I got to the gallery, I did as Newman advised. The red is so redly red that as you stand up close, you forget where you are; you're no longer distracted by what's around you, and you find yourself filled with serene amazement.

I am persuaded that this is why God retained all the details of the Christmas story around us. We are so quickly forgetful. We can be so easily distracted. The further we stand away from the Christmas story the less we are gripped with the life-changing wonder of knowing that God became a child so that we would be no longer be separate from God, but would be now and forever the children of God. You and I need to get so close to this story that it envelops and changes us. We need to get so close to this story that it overwhelms any other defining story that we have carried around with us. We need to get up close so we can hear the song of the angels and feel the fearful, excited wonder of the shepherds. We need to get up close so we can sense the amazement of Mary and Joseph as they grasp to understand what it means that their baby boy was born by the Holy Spirit to Mary, who was still a virgin. You and I need to get up close to the Christmas story so we can look into the manger at the baby Jesus and consider the fact that in the manger lies One who is fully God and fully baby boy.

Tomorrow you will reach for a story to make sense out of what is happening in your story. Tomorrow you will use that story as your interpretive tool more times than you will be aware. My prayer is that the story you will reach for will be the story of how God became a man so that we who were alienated and separated from him would become his children. And my prayer is that as you live with the glory of a birth-of-Jesus mentality, it will cause you to carry with you the security of a child-of-God identity.

For further study: 1 John 3:1–3

For parents and children:
Central theme: Story
Ask your children to tell you what a story is. Ask them to tell you what their favorite story is and why it is their favorite story. Tell them that one of the reasons we like stories is because they help us understand the story of our own lives. Ask one of your children to tell the story of his life as if no one in the room knew him. Then tell him that the Christmas story

is the most important story ever, and that because it is, it is meant to be the story that helps us make sense out of the story of our lives. God's story tells us who we are and who God is, and it tells us of the new identity, "the children of God," that he gives everyone who believes in him.

December 31

Jesus was born to this world because what he came to do was desperately needed and could not be done any other way.

The disease infected every one of us. This condition was fatal, and there was nothing any of us could do to escape it or defeat it. This universal, inescapable plague is sin. It left us all in a state of deception, dysfunction, separation from God, and rebellion, and we were all under judgment. But God was not willing for us to remain in this state of lostness and doom, so he sent us a Savior, Christ the Lord. He was born to live like we could never live, to die the death that we should have died, to rise from the tomb, conquering sin and death, and then to ascend to the Father and rule over all things for our sake. The Christmas story is the ultimate rescue story. People require rescue when they are in a state of danger and are not able to effect their own escape.

As you celebrate during this season by reflecting on Christ's birth, consider these words:

as it is written:

> "None is righteous, no, not one;
> no one understands;
> no one seeks for God.
> All have turned aside; together they have become worthless;
> no one does good,
> not even one."
> "Their throat is an open grave;
> they use their tongues to deceive."
> "The venom of asps is under their lips."
> "Their mouth is full of curses and bitterness."
> "Their feet are swift to shed blood;
> in their paths are ruin and misery,
> and the way of peace they have not known."
> "There is no fear of God before their eyes."

Now we know that whatever the law says it speaks to those who are under the law, so that every mouth may be stopped, and the whole world may be held accountable to God. For by works of the law no human being will be justified in his sight, since through the law comes knowledge of sin.

But now the righteousness of God has been manifested apart from the law, although the Law and the Prophets bear witness to it—the righteousness of God through faith in Jesus Christ for all who believe. For there

> is no distinction: for all have sinned and fall short of the glory of God. (Rom. 3:10–23)

What a dark and dire description of our condition apart from the life, death, and resurrection of that baby in the manger! Now consider these words:

> For while we were still weak, at the right time Christ died for the ungodly. For one will scarcely die for a righteous person—though perhaps for a good person one would dare even to die—but God shows his love for us in that while we were still sinners, Christ died for us. Since, therefore, we have now been justified by his blood, much more shall we be saved by him from the wrath of God. For if while we were enemies we were reconciled to God by the death of his Son, much more, now that we are reconciled, shall we be saved by his life. More than that, we also rejoice in God through our Lord Jesus Christ, through whom we have now received reconciliation. (Rom. 5:6–11)

That baby in the manger was born for our justification and our reconciliation to God. On our own we had no ability to achieve these; that's why God graciously gave us the gift of his Son. So, what should our response be this Christmas? Consider these words:

> Then what becomes of our boasting? It is excluded. By what kind of law? By a law of works? No, but by the law of faith. For we hold that one is justified by faith apart from

> works of the law. Or is God the God of Jews only? Is he not the God of Gentiles also? Yes, of Gentiles also, since God is one—who will justify the circumcised by faith and the uncircumcised through faith. (Rom. 3:27–30)

Every day of your life, you preach some kind of gospel to yourself. My prayer is that the gospel that is preached to you through every element of the Christmas story, will be the gospel that you preach to yourself as you face the opportunities, responsibilities, temptations, danger, struggles, and blessings of your life as a child of God in this broken world. What do you preach to yourself when you are blessed? A gospel of your glory or of God's grace? What kind of gospel do you preach to yourself when you are facing the unwanted, the unexpected, the unplanned, the disappointing, and the difficult? Do you preach a Christless gospel that leaves you feeling alone and overwhelmed, or the gospel of his presence, power, promises, and grace?

When someone rejects you or mistreats you, what do you preach to yourself? When you are physically sick or feeling weak, what do you preach to yourself? When you are lacking in resources, what gospel do you preach to yourself? May the glorious gospel that is preached to you in the birth of Jesus be the gospel that you preach to yourself day after day until you are on the other side, forever with the One who was born to provide what you would never, ever be able to provide for yourself.

For further study: 1 John 1

For parents and children:

Central theme: Disease

Ask your children what they think it means to be sick. Ask them if they know what a *disease* is (a disease is a sickness that keeps the body from doing what it's normally meant to do). Tell them that when we are sick, we either need a doctor to help us or we need medicine that will make us feel better. Then tell them that on Christmas Jesus came because we all suffer from the same disease, and that disease is called sin. Because we are all sin-sick, we cannot do what God created us to do. Jesus came because he is the only medicine that can cure our sin sickness and make us spiritually healthy. That's something worth celebrating!

Scripture Index

Genesis
3 64
3:1–7 117
3:8–13 42
22:18 23

Numbers
24:17 23

Psalms
14 121
22:26 135
33:7 124
67:4 125
95 114

Proverbs
21:1 125

Isaiah
7:14 23
7:14–15 76
9:6–7 72
53 79
55:1–2 136

Jeremiah
14:22 124
31:15 23

Daniel
4:34–35 126

Hosea
11:1 23

Micah
5:1–6 25
5:2 23

Matthew
2:13 23
2:16–18 23
4:1–11 119
6:9–10 68
6:19–33 57
20:28 78

Luke
2:13–14 .... 17, 18
18:9–14 101

22:19 136
24:24–25 81
24:46–49 81

John
6:1–14 136
6:27 136
6:35 136
14:1–14 52
14:6 50
14:9 51

Acts
17:26 125

Romans
3:10–23 151
3:23 60
3:27–30 152
5:1–5 93
5:6–11 .... 62, 151
8:18–39 107
8:31–39 104

1 Corinthians
1:20–31 123
11:23–26 137

2 Corinthians
5:14–15 83
5:14–16 70
5:15 45
5:17–21 36

Galatians
2:19–21 132
4:4–7 66

Ephesians
2:1–2 52
2:1–9 130
2:1–10 33
2:11–22 44
2:12 32
5:18–19 114
6:10–20 119

Philippians
2 87
2:1–11 128
2:5–8 85
3:1–11 102
3:12–20 48

Colossians
3:16 114

Titus
3:1–11 123

Hebrews
1:1–4 40
12:1–3 21

James
1:22–24 97
1:24 99
4:1–10 84

1 Peter
1:3–5 89

2 Peter
1:3 140
1:3–9 143

1 John
1.....153
3:1–3.....147

Revelation
5:8–11.....17
19:1.....28
19:1–10.....29
19:6–7.....28
19:9.....137

365 Gospel-Centered Devotions

from Paul David Tripp

For more information, visit crossway.org.

PAUL TRIPP MINISTRIES

Paul Tripp Ministries connects the transforming power of Jesus Christ to everyday life through encouraging articles, videos, sermons, devotionals, and more—all available online and on social media.

PaulTripp.com

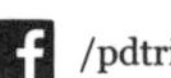 /pdtripp  @paultripp  @paultrippquotes